BABBITY BOWSTER
—— AND ——
THE CHOCOLATE TEARDROPS

BABBITY BOWSTER
AND
THE CHOCOLATE TEARDROPS

JOE LIVINGSTON

LitPrime Solutions
21250 Hawthorne Blvd
Suite 500, Torrance, CA 90503
www.litprime.com
Phone: 1-800-981-9893

© 2021 Joe Livingston. All rights reserved.

No part of this book may be reproduced, stored in a retricval system, or transmitted by any means without the written permission of the author.

Published by LitPrime Solutions   09/22/2021

ISBN: 978-1-954886-85-8(sc)
ISBN: 978-1-954886-86-5(e)

Library of Congress Control Number: 2021911332

Any people depicted in stock imagery provided by iStock are models, and such images are being used for illustrative purposes only.

Certain stock imagery © iStock.

Because of the dynamic nature of the Internet, any web addresses or links contained in this book may have changed since publication and may no longer be valid. The views expressed in this work are solely those of the author and do not necessarily reflect the views of the publisher, and the publisher hereby disclaims any responsibility for them.

This book is dedicated to the unsung and silent exorcists -
who fight evil - spiritually,- on a daily basis -
They are the real heroes of Modern Society.

CONTENTS

VOLUME 1

Chapter 1. Horror 1
Chapter 2. Glistening shoreline 3
Chapter 3. Where? 7
Chapter 4. Coco nuts and bananas 14
Chapter 5. Hennesey awakes 16
Chapter 6. A million lost eyes 19
Chapter 7. Both Minds Collide 21
Chapter 8. A mesmerising sea 24
Chapter 9. The bubble bursts 25
Chapter 10. The truth hurts 31
Chapter 11. Good against evil 33
Chapter 12. All is forgiven 37

VOLUME 2

Chapter 1. In-flight thoughts 41
Chapter 2. Meeting the gang again 43
Chapter 3. Risen 53
Chapter 4. Purple rain 55
Chapter 5. Interesting encounter 57
Chapter 6. The meeting 59
Chapter 7. Evil personified 66
Chapter 8. Fifteenth century muskets 70
Chapter 9. Carnival time 77
Chapter 10. Revival 81
Chapter 11. Seychelles calling 90

Chapter 12. Disclosure 96

VOLUME 3

Chapter 1. The start 105
Chapter 2. The Mackenzie Poltergeist 109
Chapter 3. Internal Voice 113
Chapter 4. Tel Aviv and beyond 119
Chapter 5. Shaken to the core 121
Chapter 6. War and Peace 125
Chapter 7. Gethsemene 130
Chapter 8. The Going gets tough 134
Chapter 9. A name from the past 137
Chapter 10. There is power in the name of Jesus 141
Chapter 11. The dark side 151

VOLUME 4

Chapter 1. Rising 157
Chapter 2. Ida Peerdeman 160
Chapter 3. More missing people 162
Chapter 4. Preparation time 164
Chapter 5. Amsterdam 166
Chapter 6. Disclosure 171
Chapter 7. A new dawn 175
Chapter 8. The Crickles of Cricklewood 179
Chapter 9. All hell breaks loose 182
Chapter 10. A surprise waiting 186
Chapter 11. The diary 194
Chapter 12. A shock 198

VOLUME 5

Chapter 1. Opening the diary 203
Chapter 2. A chance encounter 206
Chapter 3. A luminous green arc 211
Chapter 4. The meeting 217
Chapter 5. It's only five minutes away 220
Chapter 6. Schindler's factory 222
Chapter 7. Czestochowa 223
Chapter 8. Land of the Midnight Sun 227

Chapter 9. The truth unfolds 233
Chapter 10. Tears 235
Chapter 11. Work to gain your freedom 237
Chapter 12. Last piece of the jigsaw 239

Acknowledgements. 241

VOLUME 1

CHAPTER 1

Horror

The party was in full swing.

Everyone was dancing merrily when there was a commotion at the edge of the swimming pool. A dark-haired sinister looking woman was yelling at some party-goers:

"Look at you. You all think you're so smart. I'm telling you, be warned."

Meanwhile, as I strolled through the darkness the tropical moonlight lit up the sandy cove.

My eyes gradually became accustomed to the surroundings.

I stumbled over something lying on the beach.

To my horror I realised it was a body, a dead body.

I stooped to get a better look and saw I was surrounded by even more dead bodies. Five in all!

As I studied the faces I could see the eyes were staring out in shock at an unseen nightmare. I tried to close them but they stayed open, mummified by the sudden rigour-mortise.

Unsteadily backing away from this horrible scene I noticed something strange in the staring eyes.

Frozen tear drops were locked in timeless droplets. But, more surprisingly, as I continued to look closer I could see the tear drops were actually made of chocolate!

"Chocolate", I screamed. "What on earth is this all about?"

Looking again at the bodies it became clear they were female, round about the age of thirty.

They all had good tans which meant they could have been on the island of Praslin for a while.

Here I am in this beautiful place and all I see is death. I must get away from here and try to settle my frayed nerves.

As I stumbled along the dazzling white beach of Anse La Blague, my mind drifted to the day before when I had landed on the grassy runway in a small six-seater plane. I was supposed to go to a fancy dress party in the local area but I was too tired to attend.

I remember thinking "this is paradise".

The journey from Mahe, the main island in the Seychelles, had only taken 15 minutes. As I stared out of the plane I became mesmerised by the clear turquoise blue water. "It can't get any better than this, "I thought.

I was jolted back to reality by the powerful waves buffeting against my trembling feet.

Only one thing was on my mind. I will have to inform the police!

CHAPTER 2
Glistening shoreline

The previous year in the Seychelles I had stayed at the Reef Hotel in Mahe, and it was only because I had decided to take a short inter-island hop to Praslin that I discovered this wonderfully secluded island.

I never forgot the early morning smell of the cinnamon leaves drying in the sunshine.

That was such a pleasant memory.

But at this very moment my memory of those horrible dead bodies was prominent in my mind.

It was getting late as I continued to splash through the glistening waves on this secluded bay of La Blague.

All of a sudden a black parrot swooped in from nowhere.

It frightened me. I quickened my steps and then ran along the shoreline in a desperate attempt to leave my thoughts behind.

I could see in the distance Anse La Ferine. I had travelled there the previous year. From the top of the hill near La Ferine you can see La Digue and Le Ronde, two further beautiful islands.

I came to my senses. I need to get to the capital Baie Saint Anne and the local police station.

Eventually I arrived and made my way to the small white building which I had seen the year before.

Two policemen were there, dressed in all-white uniforms of short sleeved shirts, white baggy shorts and long white socks. The room was sparsely furnished with only a filing cabinet in the corner.

A fan was blowing the sweaty air into my face as I glanced at the officers.

Sergeant Ghislaine was busy with paperwork lying on his bamboo desk. Raising his head he asked: "Who are you, and what are you doing here at this early hour?"

"My name is Babbity Bowster," I said.

Both policemen burst into laughter!

Sergeant Ghislaine, with eyes focused on my denim shorts, said: "Babbity Bowster, that's a strange name!"

"I'm Scottish. My mother gave me that name. She was a dancer and she named me after an old Scottish dance. I hope that answers your question."

Sergeant Ghislaine responded: "You seem a bit angry?"

"I thought you were laughing at me," I replied.

"No," said the sergeant. "It was your name that sounded so funny."

A few moments of awkward silence then Ghislaine spoke again: "Have you been here before?"

"Yes, I was here last year."

"I thought I recognised you. Anyway, what can we do for you?"

I spoke in a hurried and quivering voice: "Only an hour ago I stumbled upon five dead bodies. It was horrible. The look on their faces was evil."

"Try to calm down," said Ghislaine sympathetically. He continued: "Would you like a coffee Babbity?"

"Yes, that would be good," I said.

"Hennesey, go and make the coffee."

"Yes sir," replied the junior officer.

"Now let's see - you stumbled upon some bodies," said Ghislaine looking seriously at me.

"Yes, yes I've already told you that. Are you not listening?"

"Calm down son we're only trying to get some answers."

"Where did you find the bodies? "asked Ghislaine.

"Near the hotel at the other end of Anse La Ferine."

"Ah, yes I know that hotel. It has a large swimming pool."

"Yes that's the one", I replied, rather agitated.

I added: "There's a small rocky cove next to the hotel, that's where the bodies lie."

Hennesey returned with the coffee and soon we were all in deep conversation.

"Did you notice anything lying around that might help the investigation?" asked Ghislaine.

"No, the only thing I found strange was chocolate tear drops on the faces of all the woman."

"Chocolate tear drops?" interrupted Hennesey.

I took a hurried sip of the coffee and continued: "Yes, chocolate tear drops! But it was the look of horror on their faces that really shocked me; as if they had seen a ghost or something. All the woman were wearing bright flowery dresses."

"All of them were woman?" asked Ghislaine.

"Yes, all of them were woman. Did you not hear me the first time?"

"Calm down son, we're only trying to get to the truth," said Ghislaine.

He probed again: "Did you see anything that was unusual?"

"As a matter of fact I did," I said. "A black parrot swooped in towards me as I hurried along the beach."

"Anything else?" continued Ghislaine.

"Yes, I saw a dark-haired woman who seemed to appear out of nowhere. She startled me."

"Where did she go?" asked Hennesey.

"She just seemed to disappear. Yes, disappear! Are you guys loosing your memory?" I grumbled.

Ghislaine, looking sternly at me raised his voice: "Once again, may I remind you we are serving policeman here on Praslin and we don't like people being sarcastic with us. So I would appreciate a little more respect Babbity. Do you hear me?

There was no quick answer from me!

"Do you hear me son?" repeated Ghislaine.

In a sort of drawn out voice I finally answered: "Yea, I hear you."

"Good", replied Ghislaine in a satisfied tone.

"Hennesy, get the land rover and we will all travel to the scene of the crime," he said.

Hennesey marched out of the room to get the keys.

Ghislaine noticed something strange on my denim shorts, but said nothing.

He asked: "Did you recognise the woman you saw on the beach?"

"Strangely enough she seemed vaguely familiar," I answered.

Ghislaine continued to slurp his coffee.

"Mmm, you feel you recognised her?"

"Yes, I've already told you that, I said impatiently.

"Do you ever listen? I've told you to show some respect," bawled Ghislaine.

I just stared at the polished dark wooden floor, not even acknowledging Ghislaine's anger.

Hennesey arrived with the keys. "Everything ready sir," he said.

"Finish your coffee Hennesey then we move."

"Ok sir."

CHAPTER 3

Where?

"Hennesey, I thought you knew where the hotel was, exclaimed Ghislaine. "You've been here a hundred times before!"

"I do, I do," replied an exasperated Hennesey.

"Well it looks as though we're lost," prompted Ghislaine.

"Something strange. I can't see properly," said Hennesey.

"Just look for the white tower clock, that's a good landmark," suggested Ghislaine.

I said nothing. I sat in the back seat in some sort of daze.

Ghislaine looked in the rear mirror and noticed the glazed look on my face.

As the land rover sped forward the red clay roadway was spitting dust everywhere, causing Ghislaine to bawl out: "Not only are we lost, but we can't see a bloody thing."

Just then the narrow road seemed to descend steeply causing everyone to violently lurch forward.

It seemed like a dream as we drifted downwards into a haze of nothingness.

I screamed: "Look there in front, it's the black parrot that I saw on the beach."

"What on earth …." exclaimed Ghislaine, as the land rover took another deep dive into the unknown.

"What kind of roadway is this?" screamed Ghislaine.

"Maybe it's a highway to hell," smirked Hennesey.

"What, what did you say?" asked a nervous Ghislaine.

"It could be a highway to hell," I retorted.

Ghislaine became nervous. His thinking became erratic. He just sat there stunned at what was happening.

How come the other two seem to be agreeing he thought.

Suddenly the land rover began to take a steep climb.

Ghislaine shouted in relief: "Look, we're coming back to some kind of surface. What the hell was that all about?"

"Maybe the sat nav got a bit wonky, "quipped a smiling Hennesy.

With a sudden jolt the land rover seemed to level off and in the distance we could see the clock tower of the hotel.

"Look it's there, the hotel," sighed a relieved Ghislaine.

The coconut trees were swaying in the wind as we finally pulled up at the front entrance.

"Before we go in," said Ghislaine, "Can somebody explain to me what just happened there?"

"Maybe it was a collective dream," I answered smugly.

"It seemed awful real to me," muttered Ghislaine.

He continued: "Anyway, we're finally at our destination. Babbity, lead us to the spot where the bodies are."

The music at the poolside was still echoing away.

A reggae band was swaying in tandem with the movement of the trees. Some people were dancing the Sega, a local dance synonymous with the Seychelles.

"This must be a 24 hour party," said Ghislaine as they made their way around the pool to the beach area.

The combination of creole music and barbecued chicken prompted Hennesey to remark: "Maybe we can join in on the way back!"

"I think once we see these bodies we will have enough on our plates," growled Ghislaine.

Through the patio at the back of the pool we strode and then the warm sand of the beach cove started to fill our shoes.

"I hate wearing shoes in the sand, it gets everywhere," complained Hennesey.

"Never mind the sand, where are the bodies?" asked Ghislaine.

We stopped abruptly. "Well, what do you think?" I said. "I told you it's not a pretty sight!"

Hennesey strolled over to the first body and pushed it with his feet.

"Yea, they definitely look dead to me," he said.

"Wonderful," muttered Ghislaine. "Of course they're dead! Look they are solid from the rigour mortise."

The music in the background suddenly stopped as the hotel party-goers formed a backdrop of horrified onlookers. Shrieks of horror were heard.

"Be quiet," commanded Ghislaine.

"You lot have been here most of the night, and none of you realised these bodies were here. Is that correct?"

Nobody spoke, they were stunned at what they witnessed.

"Well, have you lost your tongues?" asked Ghislaine.

"It's too dark down there to see," muttered one of them.

Ghislaine announced: "Everyone go and sit down. Try to calm yourselves. I will need to ask some questions."

The party-goers shuffled away silently to the poolside.

"Now, Babbity explain exactly what happened," said Ghislaine in a serious voice.

"As I have previously told you I was walking down to the beach after leaving the poolside party …."

"Ah, so you were at the party?" quizzed Ghislaine.

"Did I not tell you that before?" I replied.

"Now I have got to say Babbity, you were the one asking me about my memory in the police station weren't you? Well…"

"I must have forgotten to tell you," I replied.

"Well"… continued Ghislaine.

I started to tug at my denim shorts, and nervously, I pointed to the dead females, remarking ….

"When my eyes suddenly became accustomed to the dark I realised to my horror … these, these bodies."

"Look at them," interrupted Ghislaine. "They are all beautiful young woman. And now, nothing. Their lives are cut short for what, for what!"

Hennessey spoke: "What's with the chocolate tear drops?"

As he stooped to run his index finger through the chocolate I remarked: "Yes, I told you that in the station and you laughed at me. You're not laughing now are you?"

"Calm down Babbity, it's seeing that's believing," said Ghislaine.

He continued: "Hennessey, take some photographs. We'll have to contact forensics. Let's look at the bodies for any further signs of injury."

"Forensics are on their way," said Hennessy as he placed his mobile phone into the wide pockets of his shorts.

Both policemen inspected the bodies but could see no further signs of physical attacks.

"What caused those horrific stares?" asked Ghislaine.

"Whatever it was, it sure wasn't pleasant," answered Hennesey.

Ghislaine commanded: "Hennesey, stay here until the forensics team arrive. I will question the other guests. Come on Babbity let's go."

When we arrived at the poolside there was an eerie silence. The party-goers sat there with stunned expressions.

"Well," shouted Ghislaine. "Do any of you remember anything strange happening tonight?"

A sudden strong wind made the palm trees almost bend over. A blood-curdling trembling voice shattered the silence.

"The meek shall inherit the earth, oh yeh."

Ghislaine turned suddenly towards me, anxiously asking: "Did you hear that voice?"

"What voice?" I replied.

"Did any of you hear that horrible voice?" continued Ghislaine as he scanned the poolside guests for any signs of recognition.

"No," replied everyone in unison.

"I heard a voice, and it wasn't pleasant," continued Ghislaine. "What the hell is going on Babbity? First the descent into the unknown and now this voice. I need answers."

I shuffled about, flicking my feet through the surface water of the illuminated swimming pool.

I spoke in a hesitant voice: "I have no idea. I feel the same as when I found the bodies. I don't know who they are and what killed them. I'm sorry Ghislaine, but I can't help. It looks as though you need to search further."

"Oh, I'll search further alright! I don't give up easily," replied an angry Ghislaine.

"Oh yeh!"

It was the same horrible voice.

Without speaking to anyone, Ghislaine looked up and shouted: "Who is this? What is your name?"

Once again the palm trees began to bend as a powerful wind blew over deck chairs and threw poolside tables high into the air.

"My, my you are angry are you not?"

Ghislaine replied: "You bet."

An eerie silence took hold.

"My name is Ego."

Ghislaine shook his head back and forward scratching his unshaven chin.

"What?" he asked.

The blood curdling reply was soon to follow.

"I will repeat this only once. My name is Ego."

"That's a strange one. Are you related to anyone here!"

"Oh, I'm related to everyone on the earth."

Ghislaine said in a scared voice: "Everyone on earth? You must have a really big family then."

Suddenly Ghislaine's knees began to buckle and he screamed in pain.

The voice replied: *"Don't be sarcastic with me you joke of a policeman."*

I leaned over the prostrate body of Ghislaine and dragged him to his feet, asking: "What's wrong with you?"

He stared back with a painful expression saying: "Did you hear that?"

"Hear what?" I asked.

"The voice, surely you heard it?" said Ghislaine.

"No, I think you're losing your marbles," I replied.

Ghislaine, looking at the party-goers, asked: "Did any of you hear that voice?"

They all nodded their heads from side to side.

"There you go Ghislaine, the only person hearing the voice is you," I said.

"I'm telling you its real," he insisted.

Just then the six-strong forensics team arrived in their all-white plastic suits and shoe covers.

"Where are the bodies?" asked the leader.

A shaken Ghislaine pointed to the spot behind the pool.

"*Ego*," that's a strange name he thought.

Turning to me he said: "We can let you go home now. We will drop you off, or would you rather walk?"

"I think after what has happened I would definitely like a lift," I said.

"Ok. Ah here's Hennesey."

Ghislaine turned to the party-goers and asked: "Did any of you see anything unusual at the poolside party today?"

A tall handsome man who was wearing an all-white cotton suit stepped forward and spoke for the group: "I don't think there was anything unusual, except we saw a black parrot flying around."

"A black parrot!" I shouted.

"The island is full of these parrots Babbity. It would be a miracle if it was the parrot you saw on the beach,"replied Ghislaine in a sarcastic voice.

"Only suggesting," I said.

"I'm the policeman here, leave the guesswork to me Babbity," replied Ghislaine.

It was time to go. We made our way to the Land Rover.

The early morning breeze brought in the familiar pleasant smell of cinnamon leaves drying on the hotel lawn. The palm trees were motionless, a distinct change from the earlier erratic contortions.

"Well Babbity, where do you stay?" asked Ghislaine.

"Just along the bay. It's a small cottage I rent from one of the locals. I lived there last year too."

"Well I guess you will be glad to get some sleep," said Ghislaine. "This case still has a lot of unanswered questions. We may need you as a possible witness.

"We will be in touch," he said as the Land Rover drew up outside the cottage.

"Hennesey let's hand over to the morning shift and get to our beds. We'll need to conserve our energies," added Ghislaine.

CHAPTER 4

Coco nuts and bananas

In my dream I had munched my way through a bunch of tiny bananas and supplemented it with a glorious drink from a fallen coconut.

I had just escaped from a screaming group of horrible demons.

They had chased me along the beach. My heart was beating furiously. Where had these yellow-eyed demons came from?

Suddenly I saw a narrow white horizontal light appearing in front of me. It grew wider and wider until I could make out the stove in my bedroom.

I awakened from the nightmare! Sweating, I put on my shorts and stepped onto the refreshingly cool marble flooring.

Did the events of yesterday have anything to do with the dream I wondered.

I shouted in a nervous loud voice: "Praslin you are truly beautiful, but the mind is a complicated thing, easily damaged and unrelenting. Even these beautiful beaches cannot erase the horror of yesterday."

Sitting on the bamboo rocking chair I slurped hurriedly at a coffee. The sweet aroma took my mind back to my home town of Edinburgh.

I loved meeting up with my pals in the local coffee shop which looked directly onto Edinburgh Castle.

"If they could see me now," I thought.

There was a knock at the front door. It was Ghislaine who said: "There has been a development in the case. We need you down at the station. Let's move."

I was a bit peeved at his attitude. I just stared out of the Land Rover window. No words were spoken.

I studied the glorious arcing beach of Anse La Blague, and thought: "Will this nightmare ever end?"

When we arrived at Ghislaine's office he opened his table drawer and brought out a picture of a dark haired woman.

"Do you know her?" he asked.

"She looks vaguely familiar," I said. "Infact, I think it may be the woman I spotted on the beach."

"Good," replied a smiling Ghislaine.

"What do you mean good?"

"She was spotted near the hotel last night."

"So?"

"Can't you see! She may have something to do with the dead bodies."

"If that's what you think," I muttered.

"Always the doubting Thomas eh."

"Thomas, what do you mean by that?"

"Don't tell me you don't know the story of St Thomas in the Bible?"

"No, I'm an atheist. My mother didn't believe either."

"Ah I see," said Ghislaine, "Let's go to the hotel. I will explain about St Thomas later."

CHAPTER 5

Hennesey awakes

Hennesey's mum said: "C'mon son you have yur work to go to."

"Mum, after what I saw last night I feel as though I'm due a day off."

Hennesey's mum was a small plump woman. Her curly hair was cut short, allowing beads of sweat to run down her weather ravaged face.

"Well son somebody's got to earn a wage. You know how we struggle to make ends meet."

"Yea Ma, you're always reminding me," replied Hennesey as he dragged himself out of bed.

He continued: "Maybe we will get an answer today." Remarked Hennesey in a grudging tone.

"Well it's not very pleasant knowing there is a murderer on the rampage. Is it?"

"Yea Ma, it's not a very nice situation."

Hennesey dressed quickly and after breakfast of cereal and coffee he said farewell to his mum and jumped into his car.

As he sped through the narrow roadway his mind wandered back to the horrible events of the previous evening.

"I've been on a few cases but this one takes the biscuit. Five bodies!" he muttered under his breath.

The red soil on the narrow roadway was clogging up the wheel treads. Hennesey could feel the steering getting a bit more difficult.

"I better take it easy," he uttered.

His thoughts were suddenly interrupted! He screamed: "What the ……."

There straight in front of him was a group of strange looking people.

Some looked as though they were frozen in time, almost like the walking dead. Others just sat in a catatonic state, not moving.

"Is it drugs?" thought Hennesey. "What the hell is going on?"

"No, it's not drugs," said a voice.

Hennesey slammed on the brakes and jumped out of the car.

He bawled: "What?"

Again, the same shrill voice echoed: *"I said it's not drugs."*

Hennesey began to feel light headed. Was this all a dream, he thought?

"No, it's not a dream. I'm in charge of everything that is happening," replied the eerie voice in response to Hennesey's thoughts.

"These people are mine. Do you hear me?"

Hennesey replied cheekily: "They are certainly not mine."

"Oh, you feel a little bit sarcastic do you? Here take this."

Hennesey was thrown to the ground in convulsions, rolling around the pathway turning over and over again. His brilliant white police suit was now completely covered with the crimson red soil of the roadway dust.

"Do you still feel like being sarcastic?"

Hennesey lay there, spitting out the red clay that had lodged in his dry mouth.

He gradually sat up and asked wearily: "Who are you?"

"I am from the other side."

"The other side of where?" he shrieked.

"I am your lower self."

"My lower self?"

"Yes, your lower self. Or the basement as I call it."

"Who are these people?" shrieked Hennesey.

"They failed to see where I was taking them so I have just left them behind. They will waken soon enough and they will remember what I told them."

"What did you tell them?"

"That's not for you to know. You will now go on a journey. Prepare."

Hennesey stood up quickly and tried to brush off the soil from his suit.

"Let's go."

"Go where?" said Hennesey angrily.

"That's what happened to them. Are you sure you want to continue questioning me?"

Hennesey paused to think.

He then put his hands up in the air and said in a resigned tone: "Lead the way."

"Ah ha, now some sense," the voice continued: *"Close your eyes."*

Hennesey took a deep breath and slowly closed his eyes.

After what seemed like an eternity to Hennesey, the voice finally uttered a command: *"Now open them."*

The scene in front of Hennesey was horrific.

CHAPTER 6
A million lost eyes

"What do you see?" uttered the eerie voice.

"All I can see is eyes, blood red eyes," said Hennesey.

"Correct, but what are they looking at?"

"They are all staring at me!"

"Well done you brainless wonder. What can you see in the eyes?"

Hennesey, scratching his short curly hair and staring again, answered: "It seems as though they have a look of being lost. I might be wrong but that's what it seems like to me."

"Well done Hennesey. Have you ever felt lost?"

"Right at this very moment I do."

"Don't be sarcastic. I meant throughout your life."

Hennesey thought for a moment, and replied nervously: "Yea, I suppose I have felt lost at times in the past."

"That's because I made you feel like that. I like to cause confusion and unrest. It causes a lost feeling."

Hennesey really began to get frightened now.

He realised that whatever this thing or voice was it certainly wasn't coming from a good source.

Trying desperately to take the initiative he shakily asked: "Why is this happening to me?"

"Because you're like all the rest. Just a pathetic human being trying to barge your way through life."

Hennesey took the bait! "What do you mean barge my way through life?"

"Let's face it, do you ever try to stop and look at your life? Always stumbling from one unsolved case to another."

The voice then raised the volume, bawling angrily: *"Yes, barging through life, never stopping to even think about your mistakes or failures."*

"I try my best, that's all I can do"

"Piss off you creep. Full of sentimentality are you?"

Hennesey stayed silent, bowing his head in silent fear.

The voice spoke again: *"Well what next, I guess you'll say, but I have solved some crime cases too!"*

Suddenly a sound like two fingers snapping together broke Hennesey's silence.

He looked around. He was back to the red clay road. The voice had stopped speaking. The bodies were gone.

He dusted himself down, leapt into the car and drove away as fast as he could, trying to evade the tortuous thoughts going through his head.

He sped by the rows of coconut trees dotted along the sides of the narrow roadway and soon arrived at the police station.

As he made his way in one of his colleagues remarked: "You look as though you've seen a ghost."

He entered the office muttering: "I need a drink!"

He went straight to the small oak drinks cabinet and poured himself a large brandy.

Gulping it down, he slumped into his office chair and tried to forget what had just happened.

"I better contact Ghislaine," he thought.

CHAPTER 7
Both Minds Collide

"Is that you Hennesey?" answered Ghislaine

"Yes its me, are you still at the hotel?"

"Of course we are. Where are you?"

"Still in the office."

"Well I need you here."

"Ok Ghislaine, I will be there as soon as possible."

He considered having another brandy, "but I'd better not", he muttered.

Even though the drink laws on Praslin were a bit laxed he thought it a better choice to stay reasonably sober.

Back in the car his mind raced again.

"What was all that about? Those eyes those horrible eyes."

His thoughts reminded him of a song from years ago: *"Oh the night has a thousand eyes, a thousand eyes cant help but see...."*

Ghislaine and I were sitting under a sun lounger when Hennesey walked in.

"What's wrong with you?" enquired Ghislaine.

"It's a long story, I will tell you about it later."

"Are you sure?"

"Yea, I'm sure," replied Hennesey nervously.

Looking at Hennesey with a concerned expression Ghislaine strained: "Well let's go through what we have regarding the bodies."

I stood up and said: "This is your investigation not mine. I will leave you two together for a few moments. I need a drink to cool me down."

"No, stay here," said Ghislaine "We need you to try to fill in some empty spaces."

Sulking, I slumped down into the wicker cane seat and began to shuffle my feet nervously.

"What is it with you two, you seem nervous?" asked an irritated Ghislaine.

Silence descended on all of us.

All that could be heard was the sound of waves rushing onto the nearby beach.

Just at that moment a tall dark haired gentleman strolled past.

Ghislaine looked at Hennesey. "That's the guy I spoke to last night at the swimming pool," he said. "He's Creole just like us."

"So what?" exclaimed Hennesey.

"It's interesting that he's here again," replied a studious Ghislaine.

"I wouldn't read too much into that. It's probably his favourite hotel," said a still nervous Hennesey.

Interrupting, Ghislaine said: "Anyway, we are getting distracted. Let's get down to business."

He continued: "Nobody seems to know who the dead bodies are or even where they came from!"

He continued: "One thing's for sure, we really need to spread the net wider."

From out of nowhere a black parrot suddenly swooped in and swiped through the dark curly hair of Ghislaine.

He sat bolt upright.

"Where the hell did that come from?" he exclaimed.

"Caught in a trap!"

"What?" shrieked Ghislaine, as he twisted his body round to see who had said the cackling words.

"Don't look at me," said a bewildered Hennesey.

"Same here," I said.

"What the hell is going on?" screamed Ghislaine. "I heard a voice saying *"caught in a trap"*. Did either of you hear it?"

"Nope," Hennesey and I muttered.

"Anyway, I'm getting sick of these strange voices," said Ghislaine. "Hennesey get a team together and search from house to house on the island.

"Take the photographs from the forensic department and try to find out who these dead woman are.

"Babbity, stay on the island until we call on you again. We will soon find out what on earth is going on around here. I will go back down and inspect the beach."

Growling impatiently at Hennesey, he continued: "Well, what the hell are you waiting for?"

Hennesey leapt out of his seat, shouting: "Come on Babbity I'll give you a lift."

CHAPTER 8
A mesmerising sea

Ghislaine took out his handkerchief and wiped the sweat from his forehead.

He approached the white sandy beach where the bodies had been found.

The sun was blazing down as he shouted: "Does it ever rain here?"

His anger began to overflow as he scrutinised the beach.

"It's like searching for a needle in a haystack," he said. "Why am I in this job anyway?"

There was no answer. He almost wanted the cackling voice to return, but there was only silence.

As he glanced at the shimmering waves rolling in lazily on to the beach, he muttered: "Let me think."

He sat down and stared around him. There was still indents in the sand where the bodies had been discovered.

CHAPTER 9

The bubble bursts

I walked into the police station just as Ghislaine and Hennesey were arriving.

"Just thought I would pay you a visit. Haven't seen you for a wee while so what gives you guys, any further on with the case?" I asked.

"What's that to you?" said Ghislaine sternly.

"I thought you might have more information, that's all."

"Well, we will let you know Babbity when anything turns up," said Hennesey as he poured out coffee.

"Oh, that smells nice," I remarked.

"Give him a coffee Hennesey. These Scotsmen know how to press the right buttons."

I took a big slurp of the coffee and asked awkwardly: "Seen any black parrots lately?"

"Ghislaine answered: "Funny you should say that Babbity, I had another encounter at the beach today before Hennesey arrived."

"You never told me that!" remarked a surprised Hennesey.

"Well now you know!"

"Why is it that we keep encountering a certain black parrot? Do you think it's the same one?" I said.

"I don't know, but it seems to be making itself very noticeable lately!" said Hennesey.

Ghislaine remarked: "Let's look at the facts. There seems to be some sort of connection between us. Why else would this damn parrot be annoying us?"

He continued: "What if there is something that we don't know about in our lives?"

I just laughed. "Well I know I'm from Scotland and I am here in Praslin supposedly on holiday. What about you two?"

Ghislaine squirmed in his seat and looking at Hennesey he tried to deflect the attention by saying: "Yeh, what about you? The other day you looked very uncomfortable at the meeting in the hotel!"

Hennesey answered nervously: "Well now that you mention it, I had a very strange and frightening experience. I saw some zombie type creatures on the road. All of a sudden I was drawn into an eerie place with hundreds of red eyes staring at me. And that voice, it kept ridiculing me. I've never been so scared in all my life!"

"Sounds familiar," interrupted Ghislaine.

"What do you mean?" asked Hennesey.

"When you were looking for me today the reason you couldn't find me was because I was also transported into a similar dark world. It was horrible.

"I asked you to come to the beach because another six bodies had appeared at the exact same spot where Babbity found them.

"Not only that, they disappeared again before Hennesey arrived!"

"What the hell is going on?" enquired Hennesey.

Ghislaine and Hennesey fixed their gazes on me!

Hennesey asked: "You were at the heart of all this muddle Babbity. You saw the bodies. You saw the black parrot first and you saw a strange sinister lady. So what gives with you?"

"Yes that's right Hennesey," I said "but I've not seen anything like the experiences that both of you have described."

"Well in a way you did!" said Ghislaine. "Remember on the way to the hotel we descended together into a sort of dark place?"

"O yes, I remember that part," I said.

"Well then, you seem to be connected, although a bit loosely, to this whole charade," answered a smug Ghislaine.

He added: "When I look at the whole scenario, one thing is certain - we're all changing, our thought processes are changing! It seems our bubble has burst and we are now seeing either evil or reality in a different way!"

Hennesey responded: "When I saw all those eyes staring at me it was as if the whole world knew about my behaviour towards my mother!"

"What behaviour?" asked Ghislaine.

"I've been treating her badly, "said Hennesey. "Acting selfishly. I knew it would come back to haunt me."

Ghislaine looked at me and asked: "What's your story?"

"I've not got a story to tell," I replied, "except that my main reason for being here was to try to get over the death of my sister who died just weeks ago."

"Sorry to hear that," said Hennesey in a genuine sympathetic voice.

Hennesey felt the difference in his reaction to the bad news I had shared. Normally he would just shrug off things like that.

Ghislaine remarked: "I feel a change too, but I won't tell you what it is until this whole episode or fantasy has been solved."

The realisation of changes to their very being seemed to be overcoming them.

"Why don't we go back to the hotel together," said Hennesey," Maybe something else will crop up."

"Good idea Hennesey," said Ghislaine, "Let's go!"

I ordered some drinks when we arrived.

Suddenly, Hennesey said: "Look over there, that's the guy who was here on the night we found the bodies."

"Who?" enquired Ghislaine.

"Look the tall guy in the white suit," said Hennesey.

"That's right he was here, but so what," remarked Ghislaine.

"Well, is it not unusual that every time we come here he is always floating around!" said Hennesey.

I looked at the tall dark stranger and said: "Well I'm no policeman, but maybe you should speak to him. He might be able to throw some light on this whole murky business."

"Yes, I think it would be a good idea to interview him," said Ghislaine. "Go get him Hennesey," he ordered.

The stranger was standing by the poolside. He looked over at Hennesey with a knowing smile.

"I was wondering if we could have a word with you?" asked Hennesey as he flashed his police ID card.

The man looked at Hennesey as though he knew him. He replied in a soft polite voice: "Of course."

As they strolled towards us Hennesey asked the stranger his name.

"It's Michael," he replied.

Hennesey introduced Michael to Ghislaine who said: "We noticed that you were around on the night six ladies bodies were found at the beach.

"Can you give us any information that might lead us to those who were responsible for these mysterious murders?"

There was silence as Michael looked at them knowingly.

He said: "I have come a long way to this lovely island. I didn't plan to come here but I was sent by my boss on an errand."

Ghislaine looked at Michael and remarked: "So you didn't know the girls?"

"Not personally," he replied.

Hennesey asked: "If you do hear of anyone who has information regarding this case will you please let us know?"

"Of course I will," replied Michael who then walked away calmly to the other side of the swimming pool and sat down.

"Well that wasn't much help was it" I said. "There's just something about him. He's almost too calm, and those eyes, did you see how blue they were?

"Anyway, at least we've interviewed him," added Hennesey. "We can always speak to him again if we need to."

"Ok," said Ghislaine, "you take Babbity back home and I will look at the crime scene again."

Ghislaine strolled down to the beach in a pensive mood. He thought about what had happened earlier.

"*A penny for your thoughts*," said an audible eerie voice.

Ghislaine muttered: "O no, not you again!"

"*Yeh, I'm afraid so.*"

The horrible voice continued: "*Close your eyes.*"

Instantly, Ghislaine was transported back into the dense darkness of the basement.

"*Look, she's waiting on you,*" said the voice.

"Who's waiting?" inquired Ghislaine

"*Who do you think, it's your mother.*"

Ghislaine caught site of his mother in the darkness and started to weep.

"*Well are you not going to speak to her?*"

Ghislaine gradually made his way over to his mother who was also crying. She was wearing her favourite floral dress and white shoes. She was a small thin woman, with long curly hair.

Ghislaine looked into her eyes and said: "Mother mother, please forgive me!"

"I forgive you my son," she said.

Both of them held each other in a loving embrace.

A voice rang out: "*Finally you have done it. Your mother will be released into a better place of peace and tranquillity. Forgiveness is a great thing. Now you can really find yourself. No need for you to return here now. Go therefore.*"

Suddenly, Ghislaine was aware of the gentle waves lapping onto the shoreline again. He just sat there weeping.

He glanced around, all alone with his thoughts.

He thought: "Now I know she is safe. Please help me, give me courage."

Ghislaine trudged gradually through the sand to the hotel poolside. As he walked unsteadily towards the forecourt he came across Michael.

He looked at Ghislaine and asked in a soft voice: "Are you alright now?"

Without thinking, Ghislaine replied: "Yes, I'm fine now."

Moments later, after he had contacted headquarters, it dawned on him: "How did the stranger know I was alright?"

Within minutes the Land Rover whisked him back to what he thought was normality.

CHAPTER 10

The truth hurts

Hennesey was in an intoxicated state.

"I've had a few brandies," he slurred. "I can't stand the pressure of all this carry on!"

"I think I'll join you," muttered Ghislaine.

Hennesey poured out a large cognac and dropped some ice cubes into the golden liquid.

Ghislaine downed the drink immediately.

"Another" he mumbled.

Hennesey obliged.

Ghislaine stretched his hairy legs and placed them onto a nearby chair.

"Do you know something Hennesey," he said, "I found my true self today."

"O you did! I certainly found the brandy bottle," chuckled Hennesey.

"No, I mean it. I truly found myself. I've been living a lie for years, but now I feel free. The truth has set me free. But it can hurt too!"

"What truth?" mumbled Ghislaine.

Ghislaine took another large gulp of cognac and sighed: "The truth that I killed my mother!

"Yes, I have lived a lie. She wasn't killed in a boating accident. I killed her with my bare hands.

"I was drunk and then we had an argument. I lashed out at her."

Hennesey stood up unsteadily and poured himself another drink. "This can't be true. It can't be."

"Yes I'm afraid it is. But before I do anything can we complete this case? At least I can say it was finished and not left open."

Hennesey was really drunk now. He pushed himself groggily off the wicker chair and said: "I will speak to you in the morning, maybe you will come to your senses by then."

"We will need Babbity here in the morning too, and I want to speak to that Michael again."

Hennesey left after arranging a lift home.

Ghislaine was now on his own. He said: "That's it. I've finally done it. Now the world will know."

After a few more drinks he fell asleep.

CHAPTER 11
Good against evil

"Did you bring Babbity with you?" asked a bleary-eyed Ghislaine the next morning.

"Yeh, he's here," said Hennesey.

"Good let's go the hotel. I need to speak to Michael again. I have a feeling he might help us tie up some loose ends."

As they drove towards the hotel, Hennesey was still thinking about the previous night's conversation. *"Did I hear him say that. No I must have been too drunk."*

Michael was again at the poolside. He lifted his head instinctively and smiled as we approached him.

Ghislaine spoke quietly: "Can we speak with you again?"

"Of course."

"Take a seat Michael," said Ghislaine.

I ordered four refreshing soft drinks.

"How did you know I was alright yesterday? enquired Ghislaine. "You don't even know me."

"O, but I do!," said Michael. "Do you remember when we spoke yesterday I told you I was on an errand, and my boss had sent me on a long journey?"

"Yes I remember that part, so what's new?" asked an irritated Ghislaine.

"Well I have come from a place called…" Michael paused and gave a loving smile before carrying on…"a place called Heaven!"

I dropped my glass onto the tiled dance floor.

"Excuse me," I said, "can you repeat that?"

"I'm from Heaven!"

Hennesey thought for a moment: "It must be the drink!"

Michael looked at Ghislaine and said: "You know about the holy Gospels don't you?"

Ghislaine nodded.

"Does the name Michael not ring a bell?"

"Don't tell me you're the Archangel?"

"Yes the very one," was Michael's reply.

He added: "My mission was to help the three of you change for the better."

"Ah now it's all falling in to place," exclaimed Hennesey. "My behaviour towards my mother!"

Michael stared at Hennesey. "Yes, now you know," he said.

And I felt the heartache for my dead sister was gone! I looked at Michael saying: "It's gone, it's gone!"

He looked at me with love in his eyes and said: "It's a real grace to have received what you just experienced, but your journey has only started"

Michael then walked over to Ghislaine and embraced him.

Ghislaine began to cry.

"You know what to do now, don't you!" said the Archangel.

Ghislaine rested his head on the shoulder of Michael and replied: "Yes, I know, thanks for giving me the courage."

I asked in ignorance: "What does Ghislaine have to do?"

"Hennesey will explain that to you later Babbity," said Michael in a commanding voice.

"Still some questions though," I said. "Where did the original six dead bodies come from?"

"Oh that's simple," said Michael. "Unfortunately, when there is great good there will always be great evil to oppose it. Those six girls were at the party that night, and they got a bit drunk and belittled a woman who was also there.

"It turned out the woman was a member of a cult group that was evil and she put a spell on them which led to heart failure and their deaths."

I asked: "What's with the chocolate tear drops?"

Michael answered: "Because the girls did not believe the cult person was really a witch some Chocolate Tear Drops began to flow from their dead bodies. It was a *bitter sweet* tear duct reaction. Chocolate is *not* real tears, it is fake tears."

Again there was silence. We were trying to digest everything.

"Another question," I said, "What happened to the sinister woman who was following me on the beach?"

"She's the same woman who cast the spell at the swimming pool," said Michael.

"She was trying to make you feel scared. That's why she sent the black parrot to all of you.

"She knew I was coming. Remember, I fought a great battle in Heaven and banished evil down to earth.

"Unfortunately, these evil beings still roam the earth trying to ruin souls. However, God is all powerful and he allows many things to happen because he is Omnipotent."

Ghislaine spoke in a low voice asking Michael: "When I was at the beach I saw six male bodies come up through the sand, at the exact spot where the dead girls had been found. But then they vanished before Hennesey arrived. What was that all about?"

"Good question Ghislaine," said Michael, Sometimes in the basement people are not ready to leave for a better place. So those men who were in the sand returned to the basement because they were still not good enough, and spiritually weak."

Ghislaine asked: "So the basement is like a holding place to teach people the error of their ways?"

"Exactly Ghislaine," said Michael, "but occasionally lost beings will still roam the earth because they have not found peace yet."

Hennesey shouted: "I know about those beings!"

"But my mother was a good person, how did she end up there?" asked Ghislaine.

Michael responded: "Your mother probably needed some cleansing too. Abba Father allowed that to happen because you had to learn all about forgiveness.

"I also allowed the negative spirits to attack all of you. God is so powerful nothing is impossible to Him. Ghislaine your mother is in a better place now."

That was Michael's last words, for in a flash he was gone!

We looked at each other in astonishment.

Ghislaine interrupted the startled silence: "Let's go my friends. I have to honour Michael and do the right thing. Hennesey, put the hand-cuffs on me!"

I felt completely baffled and asked what was going on.

Hennesey stared at me and said: "I've seen and heard too much today. I will explain everything later. Now I have to reconcile with my own mother."

CHAPTER 12

All is forgiven

I left the beautiful island of Praslin a few days later.

I said my farewell to Hennesey and visited Ghislaine in prison.

"How are you?" I asked.

"Great now that your here," he said.

He took my hand and squeezed it tightly.

"It was a pleasure to know you. Make sure you come back and visit again. They gave me a reduced sentence because of my promise to reform myself and help others."

"That's great news Ghislaine," I said. "I will certainly come back. Goodbye my friend and take care."

"Before you go, can I ask a question?" enquired Ghislaine. "A few days ago I noticed the emblem on your denim shorts with its red coloured pitch fork and a gruesome looking body impaled on it. I have to ask - what does it mean?

I told him it represented a group of people I knock around with in Scotland who all think along the same lines. I agreed it looks a wee bit sinister for those who don't know anything about us.

"It's strange, but I felt uneasy when I studied it," replied a nervous Ghislaine. "Can you tell me more?"

"Nope," I responded.

I stared at the bleak white washed walls of the Praslin Prison and continued somewhat sarcastically: "It's my life, Ghislaine. I would leave it there!"

"OK my friend, just be careful. Look what happened to me," said Ghislaine.

"Thanks for the nice sentiments," I said as I turned around and waltzed out of the prison cell.

On the flight home from Mahe to Nairobi I glanced out the window and couldn't believe my eyes! In the sky was an angel, with the clouds spelling out the words:

"She is with Me"

I sat dumbfounded, and only turned when the stewardess asked if I wanted a drink!

"Yes, a large whisky," I replied.

When I looked back again everything was gone.

"Anyway, my sister seems to be in a better place now, wherever that is! Edinburgh here I come."

VOLUME 2

(Babbity Bowster and the Mysterious Echoes From the Past)

CHAPTER 1
In-flight thoughts

As the plane neared Edinburgh airport my mind shot back to that supposed holiday on Praslin.

I thought about the dead bodies, the chocolate tear drops and the horrific events of my visit.

"Did all that really happen?"

"Did I really encounter the Archangel Michael?"

"Did my atheistic views change?"

All I knew was something really radical had happened and my life at this moment was very confusing.

I remembered my sister's last words before she died: *"You will change for the better, remember what I am telling you."*

Drugged up to the eyeballs, she couldn't have known what she was saying!

My sister Mhairi was a wonderful human being. She had a great gift for reconciliation.

I was totally the opposite. My quick temper got me into a few scrapes.

A sudden bout of flight turbulence brought me back to reality.

"Fasten seat belts for landing," said the flight captain.

This was the last leg of my journey from the Seychelles, and I was certainly glad at the prospect of being able to stand on Scottish soil again.

As I walked down the exit gantry from the plane there was a slight drizzle of rain.

"*Definitely back home,*" I muttered.

Within the hour I was in a taxi heading to my apartment in Princess Street. I have lived in Edinburgh for many years, and when my mother died I made a decision to stay.

On entering my flat I went straight to the bay window and stared at Edinburgh Castle. Being able to view this national treasure every day was another reason for staying in the capital. That, and strolling to the Royal Mile and Scott Monument in minutes.

So life does have its little pleasures.

CHAPTER 2
Meeting the gang again

I awoke early and made myself a large bowl of porridge before heading off to meet the fraternity!

I stopped first at a coffee shop for a delicious latte, but the surroundings were too bright for me.

"Time to go to the underground vaults and meet the gang," I said.

Sitting on his throne located deep within the vaults, Gash, the leader of the ogres, screamed at me: "500 pennies. Do you remember that you weakling?"

"Of course I do," I replied hesitantly.

"Well you still have 5 Pennies to fulfil regarding the curse," said Gash. He continued: "We sent a poltergeist to find out information about you. Something is not right, is that correct Babbity?"

I stayed silent.

"Did you hear me you fool?"

Gash continued: "You were speaking about the emblem, weren't you? That guy Ghislaine, or whatever you call him, got a bit too close for comfort didn't he?"

I blurted out: "Yea, he did. He said he felt uncomfortable when he saw the badge on my denims. I told him nothing though!"

"Why did you let others see our regalia?" asked an angry Gash. "It's for us alone. We must work in the dark, do you hear me? Why the hell did you go to the Seychelles anyway? You cannot run from us, you know that."

"But my sister, she died. I needed the space," I retorted.

Gash wasn't happy: "To hell with your sister, our group is more important you fool."

He stood up and leered at me.

His horrible skull-like features were contorted. The jaw line protruded out in two huge bulbous callouses. He gesticulated at me with his enormous muscular arms: "Look at me," he screamed.

I tried to look away.

"Look at me," he insisted.

I gradually lifted my head and studied the missing muscle structure of Gash's mid torso. All that was visible was skeletal bone.

"Well, are you going to speak?" raged Gash.

I was nervous, and Gash knew it.

"I tried to keep our gang secret," I said.

"That aint gonna happen if you broadcast our existence by wearing our insignia, you fool!" said Gash.

He was 10ft tall, and the spiked horns on his shoulders made him look even more formidable.

"Look at the rest of the ogres here, they keep quiet," he said.

I studied them too. They looked every bit as mean as Gash, although smaller in height. They were scurrying around the dark-lit corridors of the vaults looking for possible lost victims.

Although I had seen them many times before, somehow this self same gang of ogres looked even more frightening.

"I know your thoughts too," continued Gash. "They seem more frightening because you have let your guard down. Haven't you?"

He became impatient; a horrible sulphur-smelling nose drip ran down his bony angular jaw line which prompted him to spit at my eyes.

I tried to wipe the horrible substance away, causing Gash to get even more angry. He screamed: "Look at my loyal ogres, look at them!"

I glanced sheepishly at them.

The three ogres were named after tiny lanes or closes which existed before South Bridge was built in 1785. The closes were demolished to make way for the vaults which emerged after the building of the bridge.

"Come here Marlin, Pebbles and Dryden!" snarled Gash. "Bring Babbity to me."

Although I was fairly tall and robust the three squat ogres managed to drag me easily to the side of their leader.

Leering menacingly into my eyes Gash suddenly grabbed me by the throat shouting: "I'm the leader here, don't forget that. You have been my subject since that fateful day when you accidentally stumbled into our domain."

Gash breathed over my face causing me to wretch. "What is it you fool, can't you stand the stench?" he said.

I tried to look away but Gash grabbed my face again.

"Many years ago the body snatchers were blamed for our dark work, but that suited us," he said. "We needed victims and their blood, and you Babbity have been spared so that we can find out what the hell is going on in that weak world out there. Well, don't you have anything to say?"

I still tried to look away from Gash's horrible face.

"You know Babbity you will never escape our clutches until you have completed the curse of the 500 pennies!"

Using his powerful sweating arm and clawed hand he threw me away, sending me crashing into the damp surrounding wall.

I screamed in pain.

"Shut up you wimp," shouted an enraged Gash, looking at my denims. "Why are you broadcasting our emblem again, how thick are you? I don't believe you; you make me sick with rage."

He spat on the cobbled ground of the vault pacing up and down and swinging his enormous arms to and fro.

He looked at me and screamed: "Look at the emblem again, what does it mean?"

I glanced down at the evil insignia and blurted out: "The three pitched fork is your domain here and the impaled human being is your conquests!"

Gash fixed his evil yellow eyes straight at me, scowling: "And?"

"Well, the red colours of the pitch fork and human being represent the blood that you like to see flowing from your victims," I replied nervously.

"And," he asked impatiently.

"The black background represents the kingdom of darkness."

"Well done you idiot."

Gash continued: "Remember the kingdom of darkness is a place without an end. I will return there when my work here is ended by my supreme leader."

Pointing at the three ogres Gash snarled: "They will also come with me. Just as well I only cast a spell on you Babbity. You can leave after the curse of the 500 pennies is complete. But your next mission will really please me!"

I looked at Gash with a nervous expression. "And what is that?" I enquired.

Gash let out an evil roar of horrible laughter that echoed all through the long corridors of the dank vaults.

"Well put it this way," he said "the last 5 pennies of your curse will be used up completing this mission."

I became even more nervous, knowing this was something that was too evil to comprehend.

"I know what you're, thinking Babbity," said Gash, "Yes, it is gruesome what you are about to do, but!"

Gash began to laugh again: "Then again I'm gruesome, you excuse of a human being."

"What is the mission?" I asked apprehensively.

"Oh, nothing too bad, responded Gash. "You will kill somebody for me!"

"No, please no," I pleaded.

"Shut up you turd, you piece of shit," bawled Gash. "You will do this for me. Your fate is sealed. The curse is still in place."

All of a sudden there was a blinding flash coming from the corner of the archway.

Marlin, Pebbles and Dryden had de-materialised. They were gone.

Grinding his sharp teeth Gash exclaimed: "Oh good, more blood sacrifice."

"Come here you!" screamed the three ogres as they materialised next to their intended victim. They dragged the beautiful 18-year-old blonde haired girl into the darkness.

After arriving at Gash's side, he boasted: "Ah my friends, you have done well. She's perfect, just perfect. My commander in chief will be happy."

I was shocked at the rough man-handling of the girl and tried to help her, but Gash slapped me in the face, sneering: "Get out of the way you weakling."

Although I had so far completed all the tests of the 500 penny curse I had never seen a blood sacrifice before.

In excitement, Gash shouted: "Bring her to me."

The young girl screamed as he sank his long and sharp teeth into her slender throat.

She slumped to the ground. She was dead!

Gash dragged the body of the girl upwards; holding her by the throat in a triumphant macabre gesture.

"Now she's mine," he growled. "My master of the underworld will be satisfied."

Gash looked at me grinning: "It's ok Babbity she had no family. She was alone in this horrible world. I always pick this type of person so that there is no suspicion up above. Pity she was alone in the vault too.

"How can people be so foolish as to come in here alone," he screamed as he rifted and breathed out a foul sulphur like vapour.

The humid air of the vault quickly became contaminated and I felt sick. I vomited!

The ogres scurried to my side and goaded: "Ah, so you can't take it eh?"

I continued to wretch and couldn't stop my heaving stomach from reacting to the horrors I had just witnessed.

Then I heard a whisper in my ear: "Michael."

"Did I just hear that" I thought.

"Yes you did you, you fool, "screamed Gash. "I hate that guy, I hate him. He helped you in the Seychelles, didn't he?"

I stood up and nervously asked: "Can I go now?"

A Scowling Gash retorted: "No you can't. I will tell you who you have to kill first."

I slumped back down again, dejected.

"I'll never do it, I can't," I thought.

"Yes you will you wimp. Who do you think it is?"replied Gash.

I suddenly felt a surge of strength and replied: "That's your domain of evil, not mine."

Gash went crazy jumping around the vault and stamping his giant feet. He exploded: "Don't you dare be insolent to me."

"It wasn't insolence, it's the truth," I said. "That's your world, not mine."

Gash swept his clawed feet through the vomit on the floor.

"Yes it is my world, it is my world of darkness, but remember you have been in darkness too. So don't forget that."

Gash paced around the rough sandstone cavern. He was still irritated by my answer.

"Now to your victim. Can you think of who it is?"

I didn't answer.

Enraged by my silence Gash grabbed me by the throat and screamed: "Well, it just so happens that it is an Exorcist Priest"

"I hate him because he has saved so many souls from going to my master in Hades. He lives at St Mary's Cathedral and his name is Addington, John Addington!"

He bent down and leered at me saying: "I will give you three days to complete your task. Remember, just think back to the blonde haired girl. That should give you a warning."

"I want you to come back here every day with a progress report. Do you hear me?"

I pushed myself up from the floor and walked wearily towards the vault archway. I turned around and looking directly at Gash, murmured: "Will do."

I then made a quick retreat to the exit.

As I walked through the maze of tunnels I noticed chip markings on the sandstone vault walls.

I also saw clay pipes, buttons, horseshoes, antique snuff boxes and broken medicine bottles.

I wondered where it all came from.

Just at that moment my question was answered.

In one of the adjoining tunnels I could hear a loud voiced female guide explaining to a group of tourists:

"These vaults were only discovered again in 1985. As you can see there is a vast network of tunnels."

Pointing to the walls she continued: *"You can even see the chisel marks, indicating much hard work went into creating the vaults. There are mysterious echoes from the past right in front of your very eyes.*

"The vaults were abandoned 30 years after the bridge was completed in 1788. You are now in the area of Cowgate.

"The bridge was built to link the old town's High Street with the university building in the South Side of the city.

And these utensils you see lying around were left by the cobblers, smelters and milliners who had small businesses here. Unfortunately, the damp conditions forced them to move out."

The guide continued: *"They say this bridge is cursed, mainly because the very first person to cross it on its completion was a dead woman in a hearse!"*

I began to sweat profusely. I needed fresh air. I plodded onwards and upwards towards the concealed exit.

I burst through the vault exit door, took a deep breath and said aloud: "Fresh air at last."

The mid-afternoon sunshine was drenching the throngs of people jostling their way across the bridge. I couldn't believe I was only a few minutes walk from Waverley Station.

St Mary's Cathedral was on my way back to Princess Street so I approached the front door and pressed the bell.

A small comical looking rotund man answered. He reminded me of Friar Tuck of Robin Hood fame!

He was wearing a brown habit and was completely bald, except for a ginger fringe of hair around the nape of his neck. His plump red-cheeked face lit up with a beaming smile.

"Can I help you?" he asked.

I told him I was looking for Father John Addington.

There was a slight pause. "That's me," he replied.

I then asked if I could arrange to meet with him tomorrow.

"What about?" he inquired.

Thinking on my feet I said I would like to speak about religion, saying I was a bit confused and needed some direction.

"Of course I can speak to you," he said. "How about three o'clock. Does that suit you?"

"Yes of course, that's great."

"Oh, before you go, what's your name?" asked the priest.

"It's Babbity Bowster."

"That's an unusual name," remarked the Exorcist.

I stared at the doorstep, and then looked at the priest.

"Everybody says that," I replied. "I was named after an old Scottish dance. My mother was a dancer."

"That's interesting, what was your mother's name?"

I paused and was a bit put off by further questions.

"She was called Morag," I replied.

"That's a good Scottish name," replied Father John. He continued: "Any brothers or sisters?"

"Yes my sister was called, Mhairi"

"That's another good Scottish name," exclaimed the priest.

After another slight pause in the conversation I blurted out:

"See you tomorrow then."

I walked away with a spring in my step. First part of the plan complete, but I really needed to get away from that cathedral.

GASH

CHAPTER 3

Risen

As I walked past Waverley Station I felt a hand tugging on my shoulder.

I looked round to see who it was, but nobody was there!

I thought I was going off my head!

"No you're not," said Gash. Just to let you know I'm still watching you."

"Do you ever give up?" I sighed.

"Never, you fool."

I walked further on but was stopped in mid stride. I felt a searing pain on my hip. I couldn't move. Pedestrians were staring at me.

Without warning the involuntary paralysis left and I began to walk normal.

"You see I can even stop you walking," laughed Gash.

"I'm in control of you. Don't you understand I posses you. Bye bye you weakling. Till tomorrow."

I walked past the Scott Monument again and headed for the flat. It was about 7pm.

I was hungry so I rustled up a Scottish dish of ham eggs bacon and mushrooms and turned on the TV.

"A girl has gone missing in the Cowgate area of Edinburgh," said the Newsreader.

I sat back in my chair and looked at a sports magazine.

"Got to get my mind back on track," I thought.

CHAPTER 4

Purple rain

Next morning I struggled to get out of bed. Then I realised a giant ball and chain was tied to my ankle!

"What the hell is this?" I screamed. "I can't move."

As quickly as the ball and chain had shackled my feet, it fell off and vanished!

Got to get out and continue my mission.

While walking along Princess Street I noticed something strange.

I looked under the Scott Monument and I could see purple rain falling, but only under the monument!

Pedestrians were floating above ground level and were pointing at me!

My thoughts raced. What on earth have I done?

Suddenly, I began to float too - directly towards the Monument.

Everyone was staring in my direction.

As I entered underneath the giant gothic style angular sculpture I was immediately drenched in the purple rain.

Then a gap appeared in the falling rain where a strange looking figure appeared.

It was a man dressed in linen with a girdle of pure gold around his waist. His face shone like lightning and his eyes were like fiery torches.

His arms and his legs had the gleam of burnished bronze and the sound of his voice was like the noise of a crowd.

"Who are you?" I asked.

At the sound of his voice I fell unconscious. Then a hand touched me, making my knees and hands tremble.

The man said: "Babbity, you are specially chosen. Stand up and listen. Do not be afraid from this day onward."

I muttered as I prostrated myself: "My strength has deserted me."

The man in the white linen leaned down and touched my lips.

He said: "Now receive strength again, but you will experience many trials in the future."

As I stood up the man vanished in front of my eyes!

The pedestrians were now smiling in my direction - as if they knew something special had just happened.

Ring ring ring.

I was shocked at this sudden intrusion, but my alarm clock had gone off!

CHAPTER 5

Interesting encounter

Yawning, I stepped out of bed warily.

My thoughts strayed again. It felt so real. How could it have been a dream. That colour of purple it was so vivid.

Suddenly I remembered my mission again.

Need to get moving, I have an appointment at 3pm.

For once I will not wear my denims with the motif.

Dressing hurriedly I grabbed a banana and ran down the stairway.

Running along Princess street I looked at my watch. I was in good time. I decided to pop in to The Mad Hatters, my favourite café, for a quick coffee.

It was my escape from the reality of Gash and his underworld kingdom.

I took my usual seat next to Alice in Wonderland!

I studied her rear end as she pushed through the imaginary wall into her fantasy world. I had seen this so many times. It always made me as jovial as a foolish clown.

My eyes scanned the various toy animals strewn around the café. There was Hares and Door-Mouses, even Top Hats lying all over the place. It haunted me with the memory of some former happiness.

Now these memories and emotions surged in my soul like a storm.

The contrast in my mind was electric.

My thoughts raced to the dismal vaults where I had to be after visiting the Exorcist.

Will Gash ever be out of my life, I thought.

I seemed to be wearing my wounds like stars.

"Coffee Babbity," said his favourite waitress Alice. She was wearing a knee-length puff sleeved blue dress with a white pinafore on top and black ankle strap shoes. Her stockings were coloured in blue and white stripes.

Her lovely smile always touched my heart.

I studied her blonde hair and freckled face.

"Babbity are you listening to me?" she said trying to bring me back to reality.

I asked for my usual decaf latte and one of her treacle scones.

Alice smiled and went to fetch the order.

From the white bay window of the cafe, I studied Edinburgh Castle again. I always marvelled at the stunning architecture.

The ramparts of the castle seemed to grow out of the massive granite boulders of the castle hill.

These thoughts were suddenly interrupted by the gruesome task I had to complete.

I wondered how I would get the priest away from his residence.

"Coffee Babbity," said Alice, smiling. "Are you going to see your friends today," she continued with a smirk on her face.

"Maybe I will meet them one day," she added.

I slurped my coffee quickly, staring at the black and white tiled flooring. I replied: "Yea maybe one day!"

Alice shrugged and walked away.

It was now 2.30pm.

CHAPTER 6

The meeting

As I walked along Princess Street towards the cathedral I thought about the young girl who was killed by Gash.

She perished like a blown out flame.

Her blood was scattered everywhere, like deep red wine.

The sun was baking hot, making me sweat in my heavy denim shirt.

I trudged down the sweeping gentle slope towards St Mary's Cathedral.

I reached the front door. It was dead on 3pm.

Father John greeted me with a smile on his face.

"Welcome Babbity, nice to see you again," he said.

He led me in to his sparsely furnished study.

On the front door was a sign saying "What's Up!"

The antique dark wooden chairs in the centre of his study were spread around the table untidily.

"Sit here Babbity," said Father John "Would you like a coffee?".

I declined as I had just had one.

"Well now what can I do for you?" said Father John in a low tender voice.

I shuffled my feet nervously. I looked at the corner of the study and saw a giant toy Orang Utan sitting on an old couch. Above its head was a sign saying: "It's only me!"

Father John noticed my movements and said: "Oh that, I like to surprise my visitors!"

The penny dropped with the sign on the door too!

"Any questions?" asked Father John.

I told him I was in a very confused state of mind. I just don't know which direction I was going in. I didn't even believe there was a God.

Father John smiled. "That's alright," he said "Sometimes I believe he is not there too! God is infinite. And we are finite creatures. Occasionally, we cannot fathom the existence of an external loving Father who created us and cares for us."

"He created us?" I quizzed!

"Yes Babbity he created you. Of course this creation was through your mother and father. He knows every hair on your head. Maybe that's why I have difficulties too, because I ain't got any hair!" laughed Father John.

I began to feel at ease with the Exorcist. He seemed normal, with frailties. But in an instant his mind seemed to be steered towards the purpose of his journey. It felt like an external force was prompting him.

I asked him if he ever went outside to talk to people who need help.

"Yes only if they can't make it to see me," he replied innocently.

There was a pause.

Father John noticed the change in my voice, but said nothing.

"So how do I get to believe," I asked trying to break the silence.

"You will need to try to, at least, say a prayer," he said. "I recommend the Our Father. It's the prayer Jesus Christ gave to the world."

I said I had heard of Jesus Christ and asked if he was a prophet.

BABBITY BOWSTER AND THE CHOCOLATE TEARDROPS

Father John smiled again and said: "Not only is he a prophet, he is the Messiah who was sent by God the Father to bring salvation to the world."

"You mean he was sent for me?" I enquired

"Of course, he was sent for all sinners like you and me."

I couldn't really take in what was happening, but I suddenly felt a loving change in my heart when he mentioned the name of Jesus.

The priest broke the silence again asking: "What did you do Babbity after you left me yesterday?"

I thought for a moment and asked him why he was asking me that.

"I just thought it would be interesting to know where you went," he said.

Again, there was silence.

There was a battle going on in my whole being.

I wanted to answer, but there was a reticence to speak and answer too.

Father John spoke again: "Did anything unusual happen?"

I struggled. Father John sensed this and said: "Jesus loves you, and he will always love you."

More silence.

Then I spoke. I told Father John that when I left him I was walking along Princess street towards my flat when I was stopped dead in my tracks. I couldn't move. I said I felt a searing pain in my hip, but then the paralysis left me. And then I told him about the powerful dream I had last night.

"Oh, what was that about?" he asked.

Reluctantly, I began telling him about the person in the dream who was wearing white linen and a golden waist band.

Father John nodded his head up and down.

"Can you explain this?" I asked.

He smiled and looking at me lovingly said: "Babbity sit comfortably in your seat for what I'm about to tell you may be hard to believe. Do you understand what I'm saying?"

I nodded.

He continued: "Sometimes God will come into a situation whether you like it or not. He is our Creator and he loves you very much Jesus will reveal himself through the angels and saints.

"What else happened in the dream? Was anything said to you?"

I told him the person said I was specially chosen; that I would be given strength, but I would also find my journey difficult.

"Bingo that's it!" exclaimed Father John.

"That's what?" I asked.

He smiled and took my hand.

"After you left yesterday," he said, "I said a short prayer to Jesus. I asked him to reveal his love for you in a powerful way. I asked Him to use you to further his work here on earth. I think you got an answer to that!"

I was stunned. I said to Father that I didn't even know if I was a believer."

He stood up, and walking around his study he looked at me and said: "You have a good heart Babbity; that's why Jesus chose you. But there are other matters that concern me.

"You told me about the paralysis. That's not a good sign. It means something else has got a hold of you, something that is not good."

I stood up and started to scream at Father John saying in anger that he was talking rubbish.

I then tried to rip off the Crucifix that was hanging around his neck.

He reacted quickly, grabbing me forcibly and pressing me down on the couch in the corner of the room.

It was a surreal and comical moment as the two of us struggled next to the toy Orang Utan!

I then heard a voice: "Kill him. Kill him."

During the struggle, Father John managed to reach over and pick up a large Crucifix from the table. He shouted in a commanding voice: "In the name of Jesus of Nazareth be quiet."

Nothing happened, the struggle continued.

I could hear Father John saying: "Come back Babbity, come back."

Moments later I started to calm down, foaming at the mouth and shaking.

He released his grip on me, stepping back and adjusting his cassock.

He then asked: "Are you alright now Babbity?"

I was embarrassed, but also shocked that this sudden eruption had happened. I apologised sheepishly saying I didn't know what just happened there!

In a commanding voice Father John retorted: "I know. A demon has possessed you. That's what happened."

"What?" I screamed.

"A demon has entered you, and you will need follow up work to get rid of it. And because you are new to the Faith it will be difficult. Do you agree that I should help you? This is very important."

I thought for a moment, and said that if it would help then I agree, but I asked what he meant by a new Faith.

He replied: "Whether you like it or not Babbity, the Holy Spirit has entered your life and you are now on a path to Jesus. Remember this."

I sat in silence stunned!

Then I heard the voice of Gash: "Arrange another meeting for tomorrow, do you hear me you fool. Arrange it. Now come and see me."

I asked Father John if he could see me tomorrow and he agreed.

He said: "Here is a copy of the Our Father Prayer, say this as often as you can until we meet. I think 3 pm is a good time to meet again."

Father John tried to give me a hug as I left, but I pushed him away muttering to myself "that's a bridge too far".

I was in turmoil as I walked towards the South Bridge and took a deep breath as I entered the vaults again.

I hated the warm humid atmosphere as it always made me feel breathless.

As I descended deeper and deeper I could here the echoes of grunting, and even more horrific, the sounds of flesh being torn apart.

On arrival at the archway Gash leered at me as he ate the juicy muscles of the dead girl's legs.

The seeping blood ran down his skeletal face as he scowled:

"Ah you're back, what took you so long?

"You lost your bravery with the priest didn't you? He was much stronger than you imagined, wasn't he?"

He continued: "You know what that was! It's the spirit that I hate. It gave him strength and protection."

"What spirit?" I asked.

"I don't even want to say that awful word," he replied. "Anyway, he will be dead soon."

Just then my body jerked upwards as if an electric shock went through me. I heard an interior word "Holy".

Gash sensing this scrambled across the rocky floor towards me.

He grasped me by the throat. The blood from his enormous hands ran down my face, making me cough and splutter.

"Listen to me you little peace of shit," he said. "When I tell you to do something, you do it. Ok, got the message?"

I couldn't speak. All I could do was stare into the hypnotic bright yellow cavity of Gash's eyes.

He loosened his grip, and I dropped to the ground in a heap.

The three ogres waddled over towards me, laughing: "You better listen, dumb -head!" they warned.

Gash began to tear at the flesh of the dead girl again. "She's tasty," he said.

He turned to me and said: "I wonder what you would taste like you fool.

Remember this will happen to you if you don't complete the spell of the 500 Pennies."

The ogres joined Gash for a free meal.

I could only look away as they slurped and tore at the loose flesh. Rifting, and pushing each other as they greedily ate the last morsels of tissue.

"Yeh, tasty indeed," said Gash. He turned to me and asked sarcastically: "Would you like some!"

I wretched!

"Oh, don't tell me you are sick again! Anyway, get out of here. You make me feel sick too," he screamed.

"Remember tomorrow, be sure to return. Your time is running out."

I walked quickly towards the exit. My whole stomach was heaving.

The fresh air rolling across the South bridge brought my senses back to reality. I took a deep breath as I made my way home for a rest, wondering how I would escape this nightmare.

CHAPTER 7

Evil personified

The small light plane was being buffeted all over the place.

It was quite common for the strong currents from the Indian Ocean - to bring a lot of turbulence to the short 20-minute flight.

Sergeant Hennesey grabbed the small handle at his window seat. He hated flying, and was always glad when the plane landed.

The flight from Praslin in the Seychelles to Mahe the main island was never dull.

Hennesey tried to divert his mind during the bumpy journey.

He thought about Babbity's involvement in the case of the chocolate tear drops and what had happened to Pascale the witch.

Pascale was responsible for the death spell. But how can we prove it, he thought.

He also thought of his promotion. He knew it was only because his former boss Ghislaine who was now in prison.

With a sudden bump the plane landed.

"Welcome to Mahe," shouted Patrick the pilot.

He knew Hennesey fairly well because of his frequent flights to meet the main police force officers of the Seychelles.

"Thanks Patrick for another bumpy journey. One day we might get a smooth flight!" exclaimed Hennesey.

Patrick laughed: "Oh get off, you say that after every trip. See you in a couple of days for the return."

Hennesey disembarked and headed through customs control; he needed to try to get information about the whereabouts of Pascale.

The airport was surprisingly quiet, allowing Hennesey to pass through quickly.

There was a white police car waiting outside the terminal.

"Hi Sergeant. Congratulations on the promotion," remarked the driver.

"Thanks," grumbled Hennesey, then he fell asleep in the car.

The sun was beating down as usual.

Entering Victoria, the capital, the driver turned left at the famous Victorian clock tower and headed straight towards the Coral Strand Hotel, which was neatly tucked away on a beautiful white sanded bay on the other side of the island.

Hennesey was familiar with the Beau Vallon beach. He had sun bathed there many times, much to the annoyance of his superior officers.

The driver nudged Hennesey. "We're here" he said.

Hennesey struggled to sit up, but grabbed his travel bag hastily when the driver said: "You better get your senses together. I'll let the captain know you've arrived."

"Oh thanks a lot for that," said a sarcastic Hennesey.

The hotel had a small swimming pool which overlooked the bay. It was surrounded by palm trees except for some old oak trees which added rustic character.

The gardens of the forecourt were enhanced by giant tortoises, much to the pleasure of the guests.

Hennesey was led by the hotel porter to his room.

He immediately took a shower.

"That's better," he remarked as he leaned on the wooden balcony gazing at the beautiful Indian ocean.

"Time for dinner," he thought.

He put on his white trousers and shirt, and left his uniform for later.

The restaurant was all white in decoration.

"My shirt and trousers match the white table cloths, how appropriate" remarked Hennesey.

He finished his chicken salad quickly and returned to his room.

He lay on top of the bed and began to think about Babbity.

"I wonder if he ever spoke to Pascale the witch," he thought.

At that exact moment back in Edinburgh, Gash felt a tremor through his body!

"Somebody's thinking of Babbity and the witch." he said. "Does Hennesey not know that I am connected with the dark side? We are Legion."

Hennesey jumped off the bed and walked to the balcony. He glanced to his left, staring at the beach.

One place of particular interest he wanted to investigate was an old derelict bungalow situated further along the Beau Vallon bay.

It was rumoured that Pascale had been seen in the vicinity of the house.

She was evil personified and Hennesey was picked for this case because of his tenacity.

This particular wooden building was close to Hennesey's heart; many years before when he lived on Mahe with his mother, he intended to buy up the property and restore it to its former glory.

But as things would have it, the police job vacancy on Praslin became available. After much thought he accepted the new challenge, much to the annoyance of his mother.

Suddenly there was a knock at the door.

"It's me again, the captain wants to speak to you," said the driver.

"How are you John?" asked Hennesey as he changed into his uniform.

"I'm fine, maybe one day they will ask me to be a full-time policeman I don't like being a cadet, it's too pedantic.

Hennesey sat on the bed to tie his shoelaces.

He hated the black regulation type brogues that were supplied by the police force.

"Maybe that will change sooner than you think John. I happen to need some help with this case. I could ask for your assistance. Would that suit you?

"Certainly, anything to relieve the boredom," replied John enthusiastically.

"Ok, I'll ask the captain," said Hennesey as he glanced at his all-white uniform.

"At least the shorts and shirt are Ok," he muttered.

Soon after they were driving through Victoria, the capital of Mahe.

Hennesey loved the colonial-style buildings.

His memory went back to his teenage years and the way he treated his mother as a youth. He was forever unruly and unappreciative.

But the Angel Michael soon changed all that behaviour.

Now Hennesey was at least trying to help his mother, although it was tough for him.

His thoughts strayed again: *"It's easy to be selfish, you just do what you like. But this caring stuff,, now that is a challenge!"*

John spoke in a loud voice, he could see that Hennesey was day dreaming. "We're here."

Hennesey studied the two orange-painted front door columns of the police headquarters. He always thought they were far too big in size for such a colonial type police force.

CHAPTER 8

Fifteenth century muskets

The police headquarters location was on Revolution Avenue, only a stones throw from the Anglican church.

Hennesey and John entered the main reception. It was surprisingly bright in décor. The front desk had a deep blue marble effect desk top.

To the right of the reception desk was a row of glass panelled offices. Everything was painted white.

"Here to see Captain Gabriel," said Hennesey smugly.

The desk sergeant pointed to the first office on the right hand side, blurting out: "We know, we know Hennesey, he's in there waiting," replied the irritated officer.

Hennesey entered the office and sat down.

The white-cane chairs were never comfortable, prompting Hennesey to mutter: "Can't you change these seats, my arse is sore already. And that squeaking door needs fixing."

Captain Gabriel shrugged his shoulders and laughed: "Will you pay for the new seating and the door?"

Hennesey laughed too as he reached out and shook the hand of Gabriel.

There was a good camaraderie between them.

"Yes, Hennessey, we need you to solve this riddle. Pascale's been seen a few times around the old bungalow at Beau Vallon, but she always seems to elude our searches. There's definitely something weird about that Pascale you know."

Hennessey replied: "You know she's a witch, don't you?"

"Yea, but even then I would expect her to slip up somewhere along the line," exclaimed Captain Gabriel. "But she hasn't."

Hennesey replied: "Don't worry, we will find her. And we will also prove she intentionally killed those poor girls on Praslin."

At this point John entered with a tray containing two mugs of tea.

Hennesey looking at John said to Captain Gabriel: "Can I borrow your cadet here? I will need some assistance on this case. I'm sure he will cope ok."

Gabriel paused for a moment, and looking at his young cadet replied: "I suppose it wouldn't do any harm. Anyway John it will give you good experience for the future."

John punched the air in excitement: "Yes, Yes" he shouted.

Hennesey and Gabriel laughed. "The exuberance of youth," commented Gabriel.

Captain Gabriel looked at Hennesey, and handing over the case notes said: "Well, what are you waiting for, go to it!"

Hennesey gulped his tea and then he and John left Captain Gabriel's office hurriedly.

"Just in case he changes his mind. Lets go," said Hennesey looking seriously at John.

Both swept out of the main door, saying muffled farewells.

Hennesey then said: "I want to visit a good friend who lives in Victoria. If anybody knows anything that is going on in this island then its Bantu."

Bantu lived in a wooden grey coloured colonial-style building. His business was selling textiles.

His house was above the trading area.

Hennesey had been to Bantu's house many times, and loved to examine the exhibits of ancient artefacts that were displayed on the walls of his rooms.

In particular, he was very fond of the collection of 15th century muskets that Bantu had acquired over the years.

Hs also had a superb collection of Indian Ocean shells.

Bantu was a fellow of the Royal Geographical Society and was an authority on these wonderful sea-shells.

There was an aura about Bantu, who was recognised as a guru in the Seychelles.

Hennesey and John soon arrived at Bantu's store. He greeted them with his usual big smile.

He was a small thin man with dark skin. He always wore spectacles.

Bantu lived on his own after his wife was killed in a tragic accident many years before in Bombay.

He was born in the Seychelles although his deceased wife was Indian.

Wearing long linen bloomers and a white loose fitting cotton shirt, Bantu welcomed Hennesey with a big hug, and was introduced to John.

"Well my dear friends, what can I do for you?" asked Bantu in a soft gentle voice.

"Come, sit over here," continued Bantu as he led them through his textile shop which was laden with long reels of fine linen and silk.

It was a blaze of colour.

He pointed to his small office table and chairs, saying: "Come, sit here make yourself comfortable. Tea for anyone?"

"No, we've just had some," replied Hennesey.

Hennesey then started the questioning: "Do you know of a woman called Pascale?"

Bantu paused, replying: "Why do you ask?"

"She's wanted in connection with some deaths that occurred on Praslin," answered Hennesey.

Bantu asked: "What deaths?"

"Do you not know about the missing girls who were found dead on the beach?" asked a surprised Hennessey.

Bantu shuffled his sandals, and coughed lightly.

Speaking in a low voice he stared at Hennesey: "Yes I have heard of those deaths and I also know of Pascale. She comes to the island regularly. There is a coven here."

"What, a coven!" stuttered Hennesey.

"Yes a coven, and there are many witches in the coven. I have known about this for a while because many of the young people here on this island are being lured into this evil witchcraft.

"They sometimes meet up at the old bungalow on Beau Vallon beach."

Bantu paused before continuing: Pascale has a disturbing atribute to her witchcraft!"

"What' do you mean?"asked an impatient Hennesey.

Again Bantu paused, saying: "Can I say this in front of your young assistant?"

Hennesey replied "Of course you can. John is my helper and the more he knows the better."

Bantu continued: "She can de-materialise and then materialise. It is the power of the evil one that rules her life."

"You mean Satan?" asked Hennesey.

"Yes, I mean Satan. Pascale and her fellow witches sold there souls to the devil. That's why you are finding it difficult to find her."

At that very moment Bantu doubled over in pain.

Hennesey grabbed him, shouting: "Are you alright Bantu?"

Bantu sat up again, and took a deep breath.

He waited for a few seconds before speaking: "That was a spiritual attack, somebody somewhere didn't like me giving you this information."

A bewildered Hennesey asked: "Who do you think is responsible for this attack?"

Bantu paused again before answering: "I have a feeling it is Pascale. But there is another person far away who knows Pascale and he can communicate with her."

"Someone far away. Who?" asked Hennesey.

"He lives in Edinburgh, in Scotland. Some sort of ogre!"

"An ogre?" asked Hennesey.

"Yes an ogre. The evil one has many demons working for him. They are Legion," replied Bantu.

"Oh no!" replied Hennesey. "The only person I know who is in Scotland is a friend of mine called Babbity."

"Well I have the feeling he is in danger from this ogre," replied Bantu.

Bantu suddenly bent over in pain again.

"Well you would spill the beans you fool!" screamed Pascale from her hide-out in Praslin.

Bantu heard the voice interiorly and told Hennesey: "She knows you're here and she doesn't like it one bit. I feel she may try to harm you." He continued. "She's in Praslin."

Again Bantu doubled over in pain. He fell on the floor moaning. He held his stomach as his guts began to wretch.

In a trembling voice he moaned: "She really is going for me now. Probably sticking pins in a doll at this very moment."

Hennesey and John gradually lifted him off the floor.

Looking into Bantu's eyes Hennesey asked him: "What do you mean sticking pins in to you?"

Bantu answered: "These witches and voodoo masters utilise the evil spirits to send pain and heartache to their intended victims. And they do it very effectively using toy dolls.

"It's true Hennesey. They stick pins into the doll at specific points. And the person at the receiving end suffers the consequences. Just the way you have witnessed with me!"

Hennesey was in deep thought.

Looking at John, who had a worried expression on his face, he said: "But God is more powerful than these people, He will help us!"

Bantu nodded in agreement, but was still suffering from the intense pain in his stomach.

"Can I get you a drink of water Bantu?" asked John concernedly.

"Yes please, that would be good. Make sure it's not too cold."

Hennesey continued: "I will have to get a message to the Scottish Police in Edinburgh. They should be able to locate Babbity."

"That's good," muttered Bantu. "He will need all the help he can get."

After John arrived with the water, Hennesey announcd: "I think we should go now while there is plenty of light.

"It's good that Pascale is still in Praslin. This will give us ample time to search the bungalow for clues. I will maybe need your help again Bantu."

"No problem," replied Bantu, indicating his stomach was settling down again.

John and Hennesey made towards the door.

"See you," shouted Bantu.

Quickly jumping in to their truck, they sped off in the direction of Beau Vallon beach and the derelict bungalow.

They travelled along the lovely Beau Vallon beachhead and were soon at the bungalow, which was located at the end of the bay.

"C'mon John, now the real detective work starts," said Hennesey.

"Put on your gloves, you just never know what we'll find here."

The green window shutters were hanging by a thread.

The former white paint of the exterior was peeling off, leaving only the dark wood underneath.

Both of them pushed through the broken front door.

Inside, there was a terrible smell of sulphur.

Together, they pinched their noses. What's that disgusting odour?" asked John warily.

Hennessey replied: "It's a sign that Pascale has definitely been here. I remember the same smell from a previous case involving Babbity."

Suddenly a black parrot flew in through the open window and attacked both of them!

They struggled to fight it off. It managed to draw blood from John's face before squawking loudly, and veering away through another broken window.

"Are you ok John?" asked Hennesey, as he offered him his handkerchief.

John wiped the blood off, replying "Yeh, I'll live."

"This means Pascale will definitely know we are here," retorted Hennesey. "The same thing happened to Babbity on Praslin, although he wasn't attacked. Now we have to move quickly."

John, pointing to the corner of the room, exclaimed: "Look, it's the remains of dead animals and birds."

"It means there has been sacrifices in here. Yes, she's definitely been here. But there's no furniture, the place is empty."

There was momentary silence.

Then Hennesey said: "We will have to monitor the bungalow discreetly. It will require lookouts around the clock."

He continued: "C'mon, let's get back to headquarters. Captain Gabriel will be interested to hear about this sordid news."

CHAPTER 9

Carnival time

Babbity walked earnestly towards his apartment. He was still shocked at the cannibalism he had witnessed in the vaults.

Somehow his mind couldn't take it in.

All of a sudden he could hear loud music. It was coming from a carnival behind the Scott Monument.

"Sounds as though they are enjoying themselves. Maybe I need to be cheered up a little," he remarked.

Crossing Princess Street, he almost collided with a moving tram car.

"Got to stop this day-dreaming," he thought.

Heading in the direction of the fun-filled atmosphere, he glanced skywards. The recent blue skies had suddenly changed. The dark clouds above grew ominous.

The thunder rolled in from the west, and rain began to fall.

He ran to the nearest tent within the carnival grounds.

Everybody was sheltering where they could find respite from the pouring rain. His tent happened to be the 'roll your penny, and win a prize section'.

He loved this game as a child. Each person was given a rotating piece of sloped wood with a slot in it. The idea was to simply let your coin roll down the slot and hopefully the penny would land in a box with a big prize on offer.

The only drawback was if your coin landed on the marked line of each individual prize box, this would prompt the stall owner to shout out: "On the line the money's mine"!

It was good fun though, and there was always plenty of banter to keep everybody entertained.

As usual Babbity never won anything. So he moved to the next stall, which seemed more appealing.

"Just knock all the cans down and win a prize," shouted the rather bored looking stall owner.

Babbity picked up the leather ball and took a deep breath. He had three balls to throw.

His first went straight past the three cans which were stacked like a triangle.

His second got nearer, hitting the top can off the triangle.

"Got to get this," he muttered. He took a few seconds to aim and threw the third ball. Bingo! He knocked the two remaining cans off the shelf.

"Pick a prize," bawled the stall owner.

While looking at the available prizes, he was interrupted by a familiar voice: "Well done!" It was Alice from the Mad Hatters Café.

"Oh, didn't know you were watching," replied a surprised Babbity.

"Didn't want to spoil your throw," laughed Alice.

Turning towards her Babbity asked: "What prize would you like?"

Alice's eyes widened in surprise as she gleefully pointed to a big pink Teddy Bear. "I'll have that one," she said.

The stall owner handed it over saying: "That's the first prize to be won today. Well done."

Alice grabbed the Teddy and held it close to her face.

"That was a nice surprise Babbity."

He replied: "No problem. Pink suits you."

"Probably the colour reminds me of the café," remarked Alice.

"Yea, never thought of that." Babbity continued "Would you like to go for a coffee?"

"Love to," replied Alice.

Babbity pointed in the direction of a rust-coloured canopy with pouring rain falling from it. He remarked: "Look over there, it's a coffee stand."

All of a sudden there was a flash of lightning and a great clap of thunder.

Alice shrieked in fright and jumped into the arms of Babbity!

Babbity looked down at the diminutive Alice and suddenly felt as though he was protecting her. "Its ok, it will pass," he said.

They ran through the rain as fast as they could and arrived at the coffee stand breathless.

Alice, who was only five foot four in height, looked up at Babbity commenting: "You run so fast for such a big guy. What height are you anyway?

"Six two," he replied, trying to catch his breath.

"What type of coffee for you Alice?"

"Just a plain Americano with milk."

"Two coffees please," asked Babbity, "one Americano with milk and one de caff' latte."

The rain gradually stopped as their conversation continued.

"Where are you off to tonight?" asked Babbity inquisitively.

"Oh, I'm actually going to meet some friends. We get together every week at the same time."

Babbity's curious eyes noticed that Alice was waiting on a response.

He paused and asked: "Any particular reason for your meeting? I hope you don't mind me asking."

"Of course not Babbity," she said. "It's actually a group of people who pray together!"

Quick as a flash Babbity exclaimed: "Pray together!"

"Yes, we pray to God for ourselves and those people in the world who need help. Want to come?" asked Alice searchingly.

"I don't even believe in God," remarked Babbity.

"But he believes in you Babbity," she said.

Babbity wiped the rain off his yellow-coloured cotton jacket. He was thinking about a reply.

He glanced at Alice with a hopeful expression on his face, saying: "I don't suppose it would do me any harm, would it?

Alice laughed, replying: "Certainly won't do you any harm!"

Babbity took another slurp of his coffee and thought for a moment before replying: "Ok, I'll go for it!"

"Good, we will have to move now because it starts in forty five minutes," replied Alice hastily, just in case Babbity changed his mind.

"Hopefully we can dry out there too," enquired Babbity.

"Yes, there is a good heating system there," she responded.

Babbity paid for the coffees and thanked the stall attendant.

They walked towards Princess Street, strolling up through the grass embankment. Babbity asked: "Where do you normally go to, with the prayer group?"

Alice said: "Oh, I used to visit the Centurian Bar on St John's Road, but it's closed down now."

"Oh, that's interesting, I used to go there myself." remarked Babbity.

"Ah, echoes of your past life Babbity. Maybe the Centurian Bar has brought us together!" laughed Alice.

They walked further on past Waverley Station and turned left down the hill onto Market Street.

"Where is the prayer group?" inquired Babbity.

"Don't worry, you will find out soon enough," answered Alice.

CHAPTER 10

Revival

Babbity gasped in horror as Alice turned into St Mary's Cathedral.

She noticed the shocked look on his face asking him caringly: "Babbity are you ok?"

He looked down at Alice with a continuing horror filled expression, but didn't reply.

"Are you ok Babbity? asked Alice in a concerned tone of voice.

"Yea, yea I'm fine," he replied.

The Cathedral Hall was located to the left of the main entrance, just behind the cafe. It was fairly large with bright beige décor and plenty of oak tables and chairs. There was a large space in the centre of the hall.

About fifty people were already there, and a group was playing soft spiritual music.

"Well Babbity, this is it," said Alice. What do you think? She continued: "I thought you were about to turn around and flee in fright. Are you settled now?"

Babbity just nodded in silent agreement. He was now experiencing butterflies in his stomach, and to add to this he could hear his heart throbbing loudly.

Beads of cold sweat were dripping down his face.

"At least it's warm in here," he thought.

Alice introduced Babbity to some members of the group. They warmly welcomed him before setting out the chairs in order.

He was still petrified!

Alice asked Babbity to sit down at the back of the hall.

"I'm glad of that," he replied.

"That's ok, most new comers sit at the back anyway," replied Alice as she walked away to help with the seating arrangements.

Ten minutes later, the prayer group began.

Loud singing and chanting made Babbity feel uncomfortable. But for the sake of Alice he sat rooted to his seat.

He couldn't help but notice that some people were singing in a strange language. "They're crazy," he muttered.

Alice was near the front as she was one of the core group.

She occasionally turned around to keep her eye on Babbity.

He sat there motionless, without an expression of any sorts.

Then the group finished and the leader started to speak.

"There is someone here who recently had a dream about an angel in white linen with a golden girdle. He was told something special in the dream!"

Babbity squirmed.

Someone else shouted from the other side of the hall "I can confirm that"!

Babbity still didn't say anything.

He was confused, thinking "How the hell did they know about my dream."

The leader of the group continued: "This is the time for prophecy. And it comes directly from the Holy Spirit."

Babbity squirmed again, and thought back to Father John telling him that the Holy Spirit had entered his life.

"Does anyone have anything to say as a confirmation?" asked the leader.

Babbity sat there refusing to say anything.

Suddenly he felt his whole body being physically lifted out of his seat. Then he heard an internal voice say: "Speak!"

"No chance," he muttered.

Even more insistently the internal voice continued: "Speak now!"

Babbity started to shiver with fear and turned pale with fright.

"Speak," urged the voice again.

Babbity couldn't control his vocal chords and without warning to his own conscious mind he began to speak:

"Yes, it's me, I experienced the dream!"

Alice turned around to look at him.

She was astonished at what she was hearing.

Babbity continued: "I had the dream a couple of nights ago. I can also confirm that I was told something special!"

The whole crowd began to praise God, thanking Him for this prophecy.

Babbity slumped back down into his chair, still shaking with fear.

"Did I just do that?" he thought.

The music started up again and Babbity began to relax a little.

All of a sudden out of the corner of his eye he caught sight of Father John Addington who had just arrived.

Fear swept through his body again. "What the hell is he doing here?" he thought.

Father John walked to the front of the hall.

The prayer group leader invited him to speak.

"It's good to be here as usual," said the priest. "It's an honour for me to give all of you spiritual guidance.

"At the end of the evening I will be on hand to help the deliverance team to pray with anyone who feels the need for this type of special liberation prayer."

Father John then noticed Babbity sitting at the back of the hall. He thought: "How did Babbity end up in here?"

When the music had finished and everyone was full of praise and adoration Father John approached the deliverance team and told them: "I need your help. Come with me to the back of the hall."

The team consisted of six people, including two exceedingly large guys.

Babbity was still not aware of what was about to happen.

Father John approached Babbity and gave him his usual big hug.

He asked him if he would like to be prayed over.

Babbity thought for a moment and answered: "Yea, I don't see any reason why not!"

Father John looked at him and answered: "That's good Babbity, it's important for you to accept."

The priest asked everybody to pray in tongues for Babbity.

Babbity was fascinated by what seemed like angelic voices singing in unison all around him.

Father John left the hall for a minute to retrieve his exorcism materials.

He returned with his relics, holy water, bible and large crucifix.

The scene was set.

After a few introductory prayers, and during the singing in tongues, the Latin prayers began.

Almost immediately Babbity sprang up out of the chair and screamed: "You bastards!"

It was Gash speaking through him.

"I will never come out of him. He's mine forever. Do you lot understand this. I hate you Addington," screamed Gash.

The voice emanating from Babbity was a horrible high-pitched scream. It was guttural too. The voice was not of this earth.

"Don't even try you lot. I warn all of you I will come after you. Do you hear me," he screamed.

The priest stayed calm.

The two large men grabbed Babbity by the shoulders as the Latin Right continued. Suddenly Father John asked everybody to shout in unison: "Out, out, out."

He drenched Babbity in Holy Water.

This just set Gash off again. He screamed: "I hate this stuff, I hate it!"

Father John noticed a slight reduction in the violent movements of Babbity and asked the helpers to release him.

It was a ploy by Gash.

He suddenly screamed at everybody again: "I will come after all of you."

Father John retorted with a commanding voice: "Be quiet; in the name of Jesus of Nazareth come out of him."

Gash went crazy again: He screamed: "I hate you, I hate you, don't mention that name to me. I hate him."

Babbity was thrown to the floor in convulsions.

He writhed about uncontrollably like a slithering snake. His eyes were blood red.

Father John dipped his brush into the bucket of Holy Water and drenched Babbity once more.

This time something remarkable happened.

Babbity's body started to rise off the ground horizontally.

He was levitating!

"Father John taunted the demon: "Is that all you can do?"

Babbity's body immediately dropped back onto the floor again.

The two large helpers grabbed him again as Father John continued with the Exorcism prayers.

"No, I won't come out," blurted Gash. "I've been here for too long. It's my home. Remember we are Legion, my three friends are here."

Father John calmly replied: "Yes, you will come out and so will your demon friends. Leave this man in peace. Through the intercession of all the angels and saints in Heaven, come out."

He began to recite some of the angels' names, including St Joseph, St Charbel of Lebanon and St Anthony of Padua. Finally the Virgin Mary too.

The demon especially hated this and howled.

Again Father John doused the demons in Holy Water. Only this time he noticed a slightly reduced fight coming from Gash and his other demon friends - Marlin, Peebles and Dryden.

He shouted to the deliverance team: "Say 'out'". In unison it was repeated again and again: "Out, out, out."

During the exorcism Alice was standing quietly at the back of the group. She was praying.

Once again Father John drenched Babbity with the Holy Water, only this time there was little fight back.

He was now lying on the floor completely drenched in Holy Water. He tried to sit up, and as he did so Father John breathed powerfully into Babbity's face with a strong exhalation of controlled breathing.

Babbity slammed onto the floor. He looked as if he was dead.

Father John smiled at everyone in the team and said: "He's delivered!"

Babbity opened his eyes and looked around in bewilderment at all the strange faces staring down at him.

He stood up and began to smile.

Everybody took it in turn to embrace him.

He felt elated and free. Never before had he experienced this freedom of heart mind and soul. He knew his whole being had been liberated. He started to dance around praising God for what he had done.

Then the deliverance group began to join in singing: "We will dance like David danced!"

Father John approached Babbity and smiled as usual. He said: "Now you won't need to come tomorrow, you have truly found Jesus."

Babbity smiled back and in a humble gesture kissed Father John's hand saying: "No, Jesus found me."

"Ah, words of wisdom already," replied the priest.

"I still must see you tomorrow, if that's ok," asked Babbity.

"Yes that's fine. See you at 3pm as planned."

Father John strolled out of the hall in a leisurely way, just as though he had just left a Sunday afternoon picnic.

Alice approached Babbity.

She put her small arms around his chest saying: "Congratulations, what an introduction to the prayer group!"

Babbity smiled and said: "It's because of you this has happened."

"No," she replied, "it was already foretold in the dream. I'm only the instrument."

"Whatever," replied Babbity, "I won't forget you in a hurry!"

Alice looked at him with her large blue eyes. She was trembling with excitement. "I'm glad," she replied.

Babbity looked over at the deliverance team who were still celebrating about another soul being saved.

"Thanks, all of you. I will never forget this night," he exclaimed.

"Be sure to return to our group," replied one of the team.

"Definitely," replied an ecstatic Babbity.

"C'mon you," said Alice, "you've had enough excitement for the day. Time to leave."

The remaining members of the team began to clear up the hall as Babbity and Alice headed for the exit door.

Babbity felt as light as a feather.

He looked at Alice and remarked: "What a night, what a night."

"And you said before coming to the group you weren't sure if you believed in God. What do you think now?" asked Alice.

"I've certainly changed my negative opinion," replied Babbity confidently.

It was a cold and damp night.

The sky was filled with dark and ragged clouds.

As they strolled up the hill towards Waverley Station, Babbity shivered and put his yellow jacket back on.

There was complete silence between them.

Almost as though both of them were trying to take in the enormity of what had just happened.

As they made their way past the station, Alice broke the silence: "I've never asked you this before, but where do you actually live?"

Babbity pointed over to the other side of Princess Street, saying: "I stay in that block of flats over there."

Again there was silence.

Alice then asked Babbity: "What do you work at?"

There was no response from Babbity.

Alice asked again: "Did you hear me, what do you work at?"

Babbity finally replied: "Oh sorry, I was just thinking about what happened tonight." He paused again before speaking: "I'm a travel agent. My office is in Rose Street."

Alice squealed in delight: "I live in Rose Street. In fact, my flat is next door to your office!"

Babbity looked at Alice with a gleeful smile saying: "All these years I've been coming to your cafe, and now you tell me!"

Alice said cheekily: "You never asked me previously!"

Shuffling her feet she probed again: "How come you have been able to visit the cafe so much, especially lately?"

"Now, that is a question," replied Babbity. "Now that you have asked I will tell you. My sister died about six weeks ago. I asked the travel agent people if I could get extended leave. They very kindly agreed. I return to work in three weeks."

Alice felt awful about asking the question and responded sheepishly: "So sorry to have asked you that Babbity. I will pray for the soul of your sister."

"Thanks," replied Babbity.

He then glanced at his watch. It was 11.30 pm.

"Time for my beauty sleep!" remarked Babbity. He added: "But before I leave, I will walk you round the corner to your flat. Is that alright with you Alice?"

"Of course it is," she said.

On reaching the flat Babbity gave Alice a big hug, saying: "See you tomorrow about two? I have to meet Father John at 3pm. Is that ok?"

"Of course," she said. "See you then," as she turned around and ran up the stairs to her flat.

Babbity was on cloud nine. He whistled merrily as he walked home.

He glanced upwards and was surprised at the transformation in the sky. The moon was abnormally large and it bathed the castle with its luminous glow.

"A good sign," he thought.

CHAPTER 11

Seychelles calling

After a deep sleep, Babbity was awakened by a sharp knock at the door.

He quickly got out of bed in his pyjamas and went to investigate.

As he opened the door he was greeted by two burly policemen.

"Are you Babbity Bowster?" asked one of the officers.

"Yes, that's me," replied Babbity curiously.

The officer continued: "We have received a phone call from the police in the Seychelles saying your life may be in danger!"

"Who told you that?" asked Babbity.

"A Sergeant Hennesey. Do you know him?" asked the other officer.

"Yes I know him. Look, why don't you come in?" asked Babbity politely.

The threesome sat down in Babbity's living room, drawing strange stares from the officers. "Oh, don't worry about the décor," remarked Babbity, "I will be changing it soon."

One of the officers said: "It seems the name of the person who is after you is called Gash. Do you know him?"

Babbity looked down at his black slippers and answered: "Yea, I know him, but I don't need to worry about him now!"

"Oh, why is that?" asked one of the officers.

"He's gone!" answered Babbity.

"How do you know he's gone?" the officer asked.

"I was told last night," answered Babbity confidently.

"By whom?" asked the other officer.

"A priest!" replied Babbity. He continued: "An exorcist priest!"

The policemen looked at each other with a puzzled expression.

Babbity proceeded to tell them all about what happened the previous night. He also mentioned the horrible events that occurred in the vaults at South Bridge.

There was an uncomfortable silence, before one of the officers replied:

"That really is astonishing what you have just told us. And if it is true, my scepticism will come back to haunt me.

"When can we meet you at the vaults?"

Quick as a flash, Babbity replied: "I can see you at 5pm. Is that ok?"

"Yes that's fine Babbity," one of the officers said. "Oh, before we go I think it would be wise to contact Sergeant Hennesey. Here's his telephone number."

"That's no problem. I will do that as soon as I can," replied Babbity calmly.

The two officers left Babbity's flat in a hurry. "Need to go to another incident," one of them remarked.

Babbity sat down and made himself a de-caff' black coffee.

He was still buzzing after the events of the night before.

He thought: "Ah good, I will see Alice soon."

Quickly changing, Babbity threw on his favourite denim trousers and shirt, making sure the denims with Gash's fated logo were thrown into the bin!

Grinning from ear to ear he looked out of his bay window towards Edinburgh Castle.

High in the sky he could see the sun was pulsating in a pool of crimson and gold, spilling rays of light onto the battlements of the castle.

"Wonderful," he murmured, "just how I am feeling at this very moment."

In no time at all, he was skipping cheerfully along Princess Street towards the Mad Hatters café.

Flushed with delight he entered.

Alice came over straight away. "You look fantastic," she said.

Babbity just grabbed her and held her. "Thanks to you," he replied.

"No, I told you last night it was thanks to Jesus!"

"You know what I mean!" said Babbity happily.

"De caff' latte as usual?" asked Alice.

"Yep, that's my order," replied Babbity.

As Alice left to fetch the latte, Babbity's thoughts strayed to his early childhood. He could remember how happy he was when his magician father would take him to see the Magic Shows.

"Is it any wonder the top hats and rabbits in here set me off!" he thought. "Memories of a former happiness right enough!"

Then sadness filled his soul. He muttered: "Why did he leave us?"

Alice arrived with the order and Babbity smiled again; he always smiled when he saw Alice.

"I have to see Father John at 3pm," he remarked.

"Ok, you better not be late. I'll be here as usual tomorrow, if you are looking for me," replied Alice expectantly.

"Yes, I'll be here," he said, "how could I miss that date! Well, I suppose it is a date, isn't it?" asked Babbity in a stuttering voice.

"Of course it is Babbity," she replied.

Babbity slurped down the latte and headed for the door.

He turned and waved, shouting: "See you tomorrow."

Alice blushed, as the other waitresses stared at her with knowing smiles.

On the way to the cathedral Babbity was stopped in his tracks. He heard an audible voice all around him saying: "You are mine now!"

Babbity was speechless, it was as though the voice was speaking through every pore in his body. He was aware of angels singing all around him.

He was perplexed yet excited at the same time. His whole body felt as though a wave of supernatural ecstasy had swept through it. He was tingling from head to toe.

As he reached Leith Street, the same powerful voice spoke again: "Preach and teach to all nations!"

Babbity just shook his head: "What on earth does this all mean?" he said.

He was now at the cathedral. Father John greeted him with his usual big smile.

He had egg stains all down the front of his cassock!

Babbity stared at the stains, prompting Father John to say: "I should have been called sloppy Joe!"

As they both sat down in the priest's study Babbity blurted out: "What a night, last night!"

"It was a pleasure to be a part of it," said Father John.

Babbity continued: "I haven't felt any attacks at all!"

"Yes, that's because the Exorcism was a success," replied Father John in a quiet confident voice.

"Exorcism!" exclaimed Babbity.

"Yes, Babbity an exorcism."

"Does that mean I am now free of those demons?" asked Babbity.

"Of course, the four of them came out!" said Father John.

"Four of them?" quizzed Babbity awkwardly. He then said: "Ah, that's right - his three demon friends too!"

"That's right Babbity. Now you will live a holier life free from spiritual oppression."

Babbity sat in silence.

Father John sat in the silence too, almost expecting Babbity to reveal something else.

Babbity blurted out in excitement: "Something happened on the way here!"

"Oh, what was that," asked Father John.

"I heard a voice," he said. "It was a powerful but compassionate voice," replied Babbity as he began to cry.

Father John put a caring hand on Babbity's shoulder and asked if he wanted a handkerchief.

"No, I'll be fine," muttered Babbity.

Father John asked: "What did the voice say?"

Babbity composed himself and answered. It said: "You are mine now."

"Interesting," said Father John. He continued: "Did the voice say anything else?"

Babbity began to cry again, and looking at Father John with tears streaming down his face he replied: "Yes, he told me to "preach and teach to all nations."

Father John rapped his fingers on the table then asked: "How did you know it was a He?"

"Because it was a fatherly voice," replied Babbity.

Father John sat down again and after a few moments of reflection he said to Babbity: "I think God the Father spoke to you. I also know that you will become an evangelist. You will travel for Jesus!"

"What!" exclaimed Babbity.

"Yes, Babbity you heard me, you will do this for Jesus," replied Father John authoritatively.

He continued: "Preach and teach to all nations means you have been commissioned by God to do His work, and you will travel to many nations to do that!

"God is a lovingly jealous God Babbity and He wants you all for himself. That's why he said 'You are mine now'. You have changed Babbity, get used to it!"

Babbity paused in thought before exclaiming: "You remind me of my sister. She told me before she died I would change for the better."

"Oh, your sister Mhairi!"

Babbity was perplexed and stared at Father John with a look of astonishment saying: "Did you know her?"

Father John said: "The other day when you first visited me I asked you about your family.

I remember that your sister often visited me because she was worried about you. She was a believer, although she kept this secret from the family.

"I told her that through her prayers you would come to believe."

Babbity sat back in the oak chair and shook his head from side to side, exclaiming: "All those years - she prayed for me!"

"Yes, Babbity. Prayers are very powerful. You will get to know this as time goes on," said Father John.

"But I'm not even a member of any particular faith," Babbity announced.

"That doesn't matter at the moment Babbity," replied the priest. "You would be classed as an inter-denominational Christian.

"You will get to know your future faith through the power of the Holy Spirit. But at the moment God is pleased with you - that's all that matters!"

"Any questions?" asked Father John.

Babbity replied: "No Father, you have been very helpful."

"Thanks for sharing your experiences with me," said Father John. "And remember to visit me for spiritual direction. Anyway, I'll probably see you at the prayer group."

Father John led Babbity through the red carpeted hallway into the tiled porch.

"Well Babbity go to it, Jesus is waiting!" said Father John as he closed the door.

Babbity looked at his watch, it was 4pm, plenty of time to get to the vaults and meet the policemen.

CHAPTER 12

Disclosure

He walked easily and in a relaxed way. All of the answers from Father John were perfectly in tune with his train of thought.

He began to analyse things differently.

Defects of character had plagued him all of his life, but now he realised that to be human was the best thing.

Confusion can actually be a gift from God, he thought.

Looking back on instances in his life, Babbity always felt the need to have an immediate solution. He could see very often he wasn't ready to act. He concluded:

"When I became fully ready, the information I needed was there for the taking.

"Knowing too much about my options before the time is right to exercise those options, I tended to use the information to drive myself crazy. That's why today after my experience, when I'm feeling confused, I will try to consider it as a grace.

"I think that dealing with confusion can be like cooking – if the bread isn't done I don't take it out of the oven and insist that it's time to eat. I will now let it finish baking.

"If a clear solution to a problem hasn't shown itself yet, I am now realising that if I can trust in God it will appear when the time is right."

Coming back to his senses Babbity realised he was almost at the front entrance of the vaults.

Sitting outside was a police car.

"Hopefully they haven't waited too long," he thought.

Constables Jimmy Rae and Alex Baxter stepped out of the vehicle.

"Good to see you again Babbity. Will you take us to the scene of the crime please?" asked Constable Baxter.

"Follow me," replied Babbity as he hurriedly moved through the entrance, completely ignoring the ticket collector.

Babbity noticed the stale smell of sulphur was gone, although the humidity was stifling.

Constable Rae removed his police jacket saying: "Too warm for me."

A few minutes later they arrived at the familiar archway were the mutilations and killings had took place.

"Over there, that's where he strangled her!" exclaimed Babbity.

The officers looked at Babbity quizzically. Constable Rae asked him: "Where's the evidence of that?"

"Look there," said Babbity, "Bones!" He pointed to another spot where there were more.

He said: "I think I know where they buried some of them too."

"Ah, now were getting somewhere," remarked Constable Baxter.

Babbity located the graves of the other dead people and said: "Look there's your proof!"

There were dozens of graves!

"This is a job for forensics. Don't touch any of the bones Babbity or disturb the ground around them," said Constable Baxter.

Babbity responded: "There's just one thing,"… he said to the officers.

"You will never find the culprits. It's a spiritual dimension that you are dealing with here. I told you that when you visited my flat."

"Oh, these bones are spiritual, are they?" asked a sarcastic Baxter.

Babbity was angry they couldn't see what he was trying to explain.

He said: "Look, these demons could materialise and de-materialise at any time. I saw it with my own eyes. That proves they are not of this world. Do you understand now?"

The officers looked at each other in complete bewilderment.

Then Baxter's facial expression changed from bafflement to enlightenment. He stuttered: "Ah, now I see what you mean, they're not human beings!"

"You've got it in one," replied a relieved Babbity.

Constable Jimmy Rae looked at Baxter and remarked: "So this means we can't have a trial or look for the murderers. But what about the families of the dead people, surely we can do something about that?"

Both officers seemed to be searching for answers.

"All we have is a missing persons' file," added Baxter. He added: "It looks as though we will have to check the DNA of all the bones and determine whether they are male or female."

"That way we could at least try to match the DNA with the missing people," exclaimed Baxter.

Babbity asked the officers: "Where do the missing persons come from, or better still what nationalities are they?"

"They're from all over the world - Israel and Africa, Japan, Canada, USA and everywhere in Europe, South America and even Thailand and Australia," remarked Baxter.

"Well at least that's something," replied Babbity, adding: "I do a lot of travelling with my job as a travel agent and my bosses give me a lot of holidays to travel the world. This costs me very little.

"If you were open to the idea, and I know that the police force are always stretched for funding to set up these type of investigations, I would be willing to help you to at least try to make contact with these long lost relatives. How does that sound?"

They paused for a few moments to get their thoughts together. Baxter spoke: "We would have to speak to our superiors. They might find it highly irregular for someone outside the force to do that sort of thing, but they may just go for it."

He added: "You could always become a special constable Babbity. That would be a feasible way around the problem."

"Anyway, we will let you know. We now have to get photographs taken and get the forensics here to sort things out."

"Can I go now?" asked Babbity.

"No problem, your work here is done. See you soon," said Constable Rae.

Babbity heaved a sigh of relief. "I will contact Sergeant Hennesey tomorrow," he said.

"Good man, off you go then," said Baxter.

As Babbity left the vaults he said: "Hopefully that's the last time I will be in this hell hole."

He walked as fast as he could, until the fresh air of the South Bridge swept over his face once again.

"Time to get a bite to eat," he thought.

The following day he phoned Hennesey.

"Is that you Babbity?" answered Hennesey.

"Yes it's me, got your message. Everything is sorted here. Thanks for the warning.

"That guy Gash….." Babbity took a deep breath before continuing: "He's a demon!"

"A what?" exclaimed Hennesey.

"He's a demon, and he knows Pascale because she is in contact with the underworld," said Babbity.

It was now Sergeant Hennesey's turn to take a deep breath. He answered: "Well strangely enough we got Pascale! She visited a derelict bungalow we were monitoring. She's now up for attempted murder!"

"What happened?" enquired Babbity.

"On the night in question she and her coven had dragged in a young girl with the intention of increasing their animal sacrifice endeavours by using a human being. That's when we got her!

"We burst through the door of the house just as she was about to plunge a knife into the helpless young girl. It was some sort of satanic ritual.

"Anyway, they will all be locked up for a long time!"

"Fantastic," said Babbity "She really frightened me on the beach that night."

"She ain't gonna do that no more my good friend," replied Hennesey.

Babbity asked: "How did you know about Gash?"

"A good friend of mine called Bantu told me. He's a guru and gets insights into this type of thing," answered Hennesey.

"And what about you Hennesey," said Babbity, "have you returned to church?"

"I did go last week! All this stuff about Satanic activity was beginning to bother me," replied Hennesey.

"And what about your mother? I hope you are being good to her?" asked Babbity.

"Yes, I've turned over a new leaf there too after what Michael told me at the hotel. My mother thinks I'm up to something. I didn't tell her an archangel warned me to be more loving,"

said Hennesey as he roared with laughter.

He continued: "And what about you? You weren't exactly banging the doors down to get into church either, were you?"

"Strangely enough," said Babbity, "I've a big story to tell about that. For the moment let's just say I will be returning to church too. When I see you in the Seychelles again I will fill you in."

Hennesey spoke again: "I'm sitting in the Coral Reef Hotel having a cocktail. I'm looking through an open window. The palm trees are swaying in the breeze and there is a delicious aroma of cinnamon wafting in from the drying leafs on the lawn outside. Jealous yet!"

"You bet!" Babbity shouted down the phone.

Hennesey continued: "I'm due to fly back to Praslin tomorrow. As a matter of interest, the autopsy on the dead girls you saw at the beach is now finished. They should be buried soon.

"I bet Pascale will be crying real tears when she's sentenced, instead of the chocolate tears she forced on those poor souls.

"I will also let Ghislaine know I was speaking to you. Remember not to stay away too long. Goodbye my friend."

"Goodbye to you too; have another cocktail on me," laughed Babbity.

The following day Babbity got a phone call from the police in Edinburgh informing him that he would be allowed to work on the case as a special constable, providing he trained and sat an entrance exam and fitness test.

So everything was looking good for Babbity. Even his relationship with Alice looked to be turning into something more meaningful.

He was looking forward to more world travels, especially the idea of finding the long-lost relatives of the dead tourists entombed within the vaults.

Bon voyage!

VOLUME 3

(Babbity Bowster and the Strange Beasts)

CHAPTER 1

The start

Babbity awoke early. He looked at his freshly-decorated apartment and was pleased.

No more dark colours, only light.

The main room was decorated in a peach colour. The paintwork was brilliant white. The beige coloured kitchen was now free of the awful black floor tiles.

And the pine wooden wall units had mosaic-style tiling beneath them. The main worktop was pine effect too.

The whole apartment was much more pleasing on the eye.

"Time for my early morning latte," he enthused.

Stretching his arms, Babbity could not believe that it was six months since he started work as a special constable.

His thoughts strayed again: "Maybe it's time for another break! And that strange dream last night, what was that all about?

The phone rang.

"It's Constable Baxter. Just to let you know Babbity some of the reports on the missing persons are now ready.

"And congratulations on your first six months as a special constable."

Babbity responded: "That's great, thank you. I'm enjoying the police work and all that goes with it."

Constable Baxter replied: "You can pop in any time to look at the files."

"Will do," said Babbity.

I wonder where I will be travelling to next, he thought.

He put on his familiar denim jeans and t-shirt, and gulping the last of the coffee he donned his favourite dark leather jerkin and white trainers.

While whistling and skipping along Rose Street to work his mind was still full of the events that happened six months previous.

He was so happy. Can this feeling last he thought.

Walking past the various Far Eastern restaurants in Rose Street always gave Babbity a buzz, and he would try to imagine himself visiting those oriental countries.

"Anyway, back to the present. Now concentrate on work," he mused.

On entering his small office, Brian, the manager, informed him Alice had phoned.

"Ah, my dearest is quick off the mark today," he said.

Babbity's desk was positioned in the corner of the office, giving him a good view of passing pedestrians.

Not that he was nosey, just inquisitive!

The office had nice modern furniture and the pre-requisite world map pinned to the wood panelled walls.

Babbity was happy: "I'll phone Alice," he said, winking at Brian.

"How are you my dear?"

"Pouring coffees as usual!" she answered. "Are you popping round for lunch today?"

"I'll be there," answered Babbity "See you later."

He chuckled, and looked at Brian saying: "She's always on the front foot!"

Brian replied: "She's good for you, keeps you steady."

As Babbity made his way to the Mad Hatters Cafe, he was on auto pilot. He could probably walk the short distance blind-folded!

"Hi Alice," he shouted on entering.

"Hello dear," she replied.

The cafe was quiet, so they sat down together at the window next to some top hats that were perched against a flower basket.

"What's happening?" asked Babbity.

Alice replied: "I was thinking of the seven hills we've been visiting over the past few weeks; my favourite has got to be Calton Hill. What's yours Babbity?"

"What's brought that on?" he queried.

"Oh, just a geographical thought. It would be interesting to know your opinion that's all," said Alice.

"Anybody who knows the city well can probably identify more than seven hills," said Babbity. "But it's an interesting question. My favourite has got to be Edinburgh Castle Mound."

Scratching his head, Babbity asked: "What's the rest of the names again, I've forgotten?"

Alice reached into her handbag and brought out a piece of paper. She had scribbled the names on it "Here's the other five – Abbey, Southward, St John's, Sciennes, and Multrees."

"Well done Alice, maybe you should get a job with us!" replied Babbity.

He asked: "Do you remember the small chapel of St Margaret at the very top of Edinburgh Castle?"

"Yes, of course I do," Alice replied.

Babbity paused. He said: "I know this sounds crazy, but St Margaret spoke into my heart when we were sitting inside the chapel!"

Alice asked: "What did she tell you?"

"I think I have to tell Father John first Alice. It would be prudent."

"Ok Babbity, that sounds like the sensible thing to do," replied Alice. "Are you getting these internal words frequently?"

"Yes, fairly often," replied Babbity. "At first it was freaking me out, but now I'm sort of getting used to it."

"Father John knows best," said Alice.

Babbity changed the subject: "I'll be visiting Constable Baxter tomorrow. He's going to give me important information about some missing persons."

"That's your business Babbity," said Alice. "Anyway, you seem to be enjoying the excitement of it all."

"Sure do," replied Babbity.

"See you at the weekend," said Alice with a loving smile.

Babbity returned to the office.

He finished work at 5pm, and as he was walking home he muttered: "Now it starts."

Once in the house he prepared for his visit to the police station the following day by looking out his black jacket and trousers with a white shirt. Nearby was his radio, hand-cuffs and body armour.

Babbity loved to wear his uniform as it now made him feel as if he was helping the community.

His present mind set was totally different from the previous erratic and insensitive behaviour that came so naturally to him.

He sensed he was experiencing an empathy for others that was never apparent in his younger days.

"Thanks to you Lord," he shouted.

CHAPTER 2

The Mackenzie Poltergeist

After a coffee breakfast Babbity jumped into his small fiat car and drove the two miles to St Leonard's Street Police Station.

He parked safely and entered the reception foyer where Constable Baxter was waiting to take him to his office.

"Coffee?" asked Baxter when they arrived there.

"No thanks," said Babbity "I've already had plenty this morning!"

"I've just been looking at your training file," said Baxter. Very impressive.

"I see you passed the entrance exam with flying colours. Your fitness test was satisfactory too."

Baxter rustled the pages back and forth looking for the Tulliallan College report. "Here it is," he said. "Your 4-month training at the college was satisfactory too. All you need to do now is brush up on your media and PC skills.

"Already on that sir," replied an eager Babbity.

"Great. As you know, as a special constable you will only work 96 hours a year. You are already working these hours to suit you so I don't need to explain any more.

He added: "You will be insured against injury and expenses will be paid for your work here.

"Obviously we can't pay for flights etc, but we will try to accommodate you as best we can."

"I've been looking at some of the missing person reports," continued Baxter, "and it reads like a who's who. I sure hope your ready for all this?" asked Baxter.

"Yes sir," replied a diligent Babbity.

"Let's see now. I have a missing person report here from Israel. Are you familiar with the Holy Land?" remarked Baxter.

"Yes, I was there a few years ago," replied Babbity.

"That's good. Have a look through this file and try to familiarise yourself with the details," remarked Baxter as he left the room to go to the toilet.

Babbity studied the file.

Name, Rachael Dayan, aged 23, tall with blonde hair and blue eyes. Last known address Hebron Road, near Cinematheque Theatre, Jerusalem. Missing for 5 years. Last seen as she boarded a flight to Scotland.

Moshe Barushkov, aged 21, height 5ft 10 inches. Brown hair, hazel coloured eyes, slim build. Address, Hebron Road, near David's Tomb. Last seen at a farewell party 8 years ago. He left the country to study computer engineering at Herriot Watt University.

On Baxter's return he remarked: "That's what I like to see, someone engrossed in their work!"

"That's me!" replied Babbity adding: "How did we get the identities of these missing people?"

"Good question Babbity," said Baxter, "DNA is the answer. The Israeli police took DNA samples from the family of these missing people.

"We in turn took the DNA samples from the bones you showed us. These samples will hopefully match up.

"This is were you come in Babbity. We need you to locate these families and to give them an answer to the whereabouts of their loved ones.

"These DNA tests can be painstaking Babbity, so hopefully we can assist you with that information nearer the time. Is that ok?"

"Of course, I will be looking at the flight schedules on Monday," replied Babbity.

One other thing Babbity - you may have to assist us here before you leave for Israel," said Baxter. "Have you ever heard of the Mackenzie Poltergeist?"

"No, I don't think I have," replied a puzzled Babbity.

"Well this is a long running saga stretching back to 1679. I know your friend is an exorcist, and after what you told me about Gash in the vaults I thought it would be a good idea if you could ask the priest for his opinion."

"I won't be able to tell him unless you give me the low-down," remarked Babbity.

"Oh sorry about that," exclaimed Baxter. He said: "In 1998 when a tramp found shelter in the Grey Friars Kirk yard he came across four wooden coffins. He broke them open.

"As he did so a hole suddenly appeared below him and he fell through a wooden partition into a previously unknown pit," Baxter continued.

"The pit was well sealed. The tramp found corpses not totally de-composed. They were covered in green slime, and there was an overpowering stench coming from the rotting carcasses.

The name of the vault is called the Black Mausoleum, and to this day it houses the remains of Lord Advocate Sir George MacKenzie."

Baxter took a sip of his coffee and continued: "It is said MacKenzie was responsible for the deaths of 18,000 Covenanters. The period was called 'The Killing Time'.

"To this day there are very disturbing and mysterious cases of severe violence attributed to these lurid happenings during the 1600's.

"Some present-day cases include a woman who says she was nearly strangled by unseen hands during the 'City of the Dead Tour'.

"Another person was found lying unconscious opposite the vault. Recently this paranormal activity has increased enormously.

"Since 1998 there have been over 450 attacks - and that's only the ones we know about! Apparently about 180 people have lost consciousness during these tours!

"Inexplicable fires have broken out, and unusually cold areas of the vaults abound. Even electrical equipment and cameras cease to work in the vicinity of the mausoleum.

"That's why your story about what happened at the vaults in South Bridge isn't far fetched after all."

Babbity said: "I think all of this activity is being caused by a poltergeist! Why does the council not shut down the tours to the mausoleum?"

"Too much money involved," replied Baxter. "They reckon it's good for tourism."

Babbity shook his head in disbelief. "So that's what we're up against," he said. "There are also rumours of Satanic activity in the area. That won't exactly help either!" mused Baxter.

He continued: "Think about what I've asked you to do, and let me know what the exorcist says. I'll see you next week."

"Will do," replied Babbity.

Babbity drove home in silence. He was still shocked at what Baxter had told him. "And he queried my story about Gash! What a cheek," he thought.

CHAPTER 3

Internal Voice

After returning from his appointment with PC Baxter, Babbity turned the key to his flat and opened the door.

He removed his jacket and body armour and then flopped on the couch.

He heard that interior voice again:

'Isaiah 53: Who could believe what we have heard, and to whom has the power of the Lord been revealed? Like a sapling he grew up in front of us, like a root in arid ground. Without beauty, without majesty (we saw him) no looks to attract our eyes; a thing despised and rejected by men, a man of sorrows and familiar with suffering, a man to make people screen their faces; he was despised and we took no account of Him. And yet ours the sorrows He carried. But we thought of Him as someone punished, struck by God and brought low. Yet He was pierced through for our faults, crushed for our sins. On Him lies a punishment that brings us peace, and through his wounds we are healed."

Babbity sat bolt upright. "What on earth is that all about?" he muttered. "I really need to see Father John soon!"

Internally, he heard the word: "Rest".

Soon after he was fast asleep.

Babbity awakened a couple of hours later and phoned Father John, who agreed to meet him immediately.

When Babbity arrived at the church Father John welcomed him into the presbytery and made a pot of coffee. "This time you can't say no to my coffee!" joked Father John.

"What can I do for you Babbity?" he said politely.

Babbity replied: "I would like to share with you some dreams and internal words I've received lately. Is that ok?"

"Of course it is. I'm here to help you any time, replied Father John.

He poured out the coffees and Babbity began to speak: "First, I'll tell you about today's internal words…"

Father John interrupted: "I think these internal words are Locutions, which means the Holy Spirit is speaking to you directly."

Babbity flicked through his diary and said: "These are the words I heard, but before I begin can I say thank you for advising me to note these experiences in a diary. I would not have remembered otherwise."

He repeated what he had heard.

Father John was deep in thought. He said: "That's quite a reading Babbity. Have you ever seen or heard these words before?"

Babbity replied as he slurped his coffee: "No, I don't believe I have."

"Well," said Father John, "this is a profound reading from the Old Testament. The whole of the reading from Isaiah 53 describes the Passion of Jesus, long before it actually happened. That's why it is so profound."

"Before Jesus died?" asked Babbity.

"Yes, long before," remarked Father John. "It's a wonderful prophecy, although the Jewish nation still believe the Messiah has yet to come!"

"But why on earth was it given to me?" asked a bewildered Babbity.

Father John, standing up and twirling his cassock rope, replied: "Maybe you are about to go on a journey. Who knows, maybe you will be going to Israel!"

Babbity shook his head from side to side.

"Do you have a problem with what I have just said?" asked Father John.

"Well, you're not going to believe this," said Babbity. "As you know I now work as a special constable, and it has been suggested I go to Israel to seek out the families of two people missing here in Scotland!"

"That's very interesting Babbity," said Father John. "I think you are going to Israel for the primary reason that Jesus wants you to go there!

"Something will happen when you are there, and then it will all become clear to you," added Father John.

Babbity was stunned: "So Jesus is taking me to Israel?"

"Yes Babbity, it may look as though the visit is work related, but I can assure you Jesus is taking you there! That's why you received the Locution."

"Wow," exclaimed Babbity.

"And you've had dreams too?" asked Father John.

"Yes, a few weeks ago I experienced dreams about strange beasts!" replied Babbity hesitantly.

"What type of beasts?" asked Father John searchingly.

Babbity looked at his diary again for the dates.

"Ah here we are," he said "I seen a beast emerge from the sea; it had Seven Heads and Ten Horns. And its heads were marked with blasphemous titles. The beast was like a leopard, with paws like a bear and a mouth like a lion. The dragon had handed over to it his own power and his throne and his worldwide authority. I saw that one of its heads seemed to have had a fatal wound, but that this deadly injury had healed and, after that, the whole world had marvelled and followed the beast. They prostrated themselves in front of the dragon because he had given the beast his authority; and they prostrated themselves in front of the beast saying: Who can compare with the beast? How could anybody defeat him?"

Father John scratched his head. He said: "That's a perfect description from the book of Revelations. I think its Revelation 13."

"What on earth is that all about?" asked a baffled Babbity.

Father John asked: "Before I try to answer do you have any other dreams of a similar nature?"

"Let me see now. Here it is. Babbity read from the diary again: "I seen a second beast, it emerged from the ground, it had two horns like a lamb but made a noise like a dragon. This second beast was a servant to the first beast, and extended its authority everywhere, making the world and all its people worship the first beast, which had had the fatal wound and had been healed ….. and it worked great miracles, even to calling down fire from heaven on to the earth while people watched. Through the miracles which it was allowed to do on behalf of the first beast, it was able to win over the people of the world and persuade them to put up a statue in honour of the beast that had been wounded by the sword and still lived."

Babbity paused and then continued:

"It was allowed to breathe life into this statue, so that the statue of the beast was able to speak and to have anyone who refused to worship the statue of the beast put to death. He compelled everyone, small and great, rich and poor, slave and citizen, to be branded on the right hand or on the forehead, and made it illegal for anyone to buy or sell anything, unless he had been branded with the name of the beast or with the number of its name."

"The dream ended there, but just as I woke up I heard the number 666," added Babbity.

Father John stood up and fidgeted with the crucifix that was hanging round his neck. He said: "Once again Babbity that is a perfect description of the second part of Revelation 13 beginning at verse 11.

"These readings are probably the hardest in bible theology to understand. There has been many connotations as to the exact meaning of the revelations.

"But to the best of my knowledge we can sum things up like this - the beast is the embodiment of evil; combining all four beasts of the evil empires mentioned in Deuteronomy 7.

"Each head crowned as an emperor with the blasphemous divine titles assumed by the Roman emperors. It is also a parody of Christ.

"The recovery from death could represent either the recovery of the Principality after the disastrous year AD 69 of the four emperors, or the persistent rumour that the emperor Nero had come back to life after his suicide in AD 68."

Father John took a breather and asked Babbity to stay with his interpretation for the moment.

"Yes, I'm sort of getting the picture you're painting," said Babbity.

"Good," said Father John. "Then I'll continue…… the second beast, the false prophet able to work miracles, is a parody of the charism's at work in the church. It demands ownership and dominates commerce. It stands for the emperor worship ; which was the badge of loyalty to Rome. The right to be a centre for the imperial cult was an envied privilege for any city."

Gulping his coffee Father John added: "Don't worry if you are a bit bemused. A lot of theologians can be too!"

Babbity answered: "I'm sure all this information will eventually enlighten my lack of theology."

"It sure will Babbity, said Father John. "The Good Lord is revealing all this to you because of your innocence!"

"My innocence!" queried Babbity.

Father John laughed and said: "Yes, your innocence and openness to God's word is obviously paying dividends Babbity. The Holy Spirit is endowing you with the gifts of supernatural dreams and prophecy.

"Many more gifts will be given to you, but in stages. You cannot get too much information at the start or you truly would go off your rocker! God knows what He is doing."

Babbity looked at his watch. It was 5pm. He said: "I need to get to the cafe before it closes; Alice will be wondering what has happened to me."

He continued: "Oh, I nearly forgot; I have a question to ask you. Constable Baxter wanted to know certain things about the Mackenzie Poltergeist."

"What's the questions?" asked Father John curiously.

"I think the police are a bit confused as to what type of activity is caused by the different demons. For instance, what does poltergeist mean?" asked Babbity.

"Poltergeist is German," said Father John. "Polter means 'create a disturbance' and geist means 'ghost or spirit'. So it's a spirit that causes disturbance."

"Thanks for that Father, said Babbity. "So all the incidents of actual body harm at the mausoleum, what would you say was causing that?"

Father John replied: "If it's bodily harm, it's a satanic spirit. A poltergeist spirit normally tries to cause havoc. For instance, moving objects.

"Very rarely is their bodily harm, unless someone is hurt by flying cups or something!

"These demonic spirits will be inter-active and quite often work together. Remember Satan's workers are Legion and will stop at nothing to bring souls to hell."

Babbity, fidgeting with his cup, asked: "What would be your advice regarding these Ghost Tours given the go-ahead by the council?"

Father John had no hesitation in answering: "I would close it down. Demonic activity is so ingrained in a place it is almost impossible to remove. The only answer is to leave it to God and let his Divine Mercy deal with it."

Babbity sat in silence, trying to adjust his mind to all the information he had received.

Father John spoke again: "Never mind Babbity, all will be well. Jesus is looking after you. He has given you a good memory to remember the dreams.

"It would appear that you also have a strong link to the Old Testament. As I have said, this will become known to you through time."

Father John smiled and gave Babbity a big hug. "Remember to come back and see me soon, and let me know when you are going to Israel," he said.

"I sure will Father John. God bless you and thank you for your valuable help today," remarked Babbity as he left the presbytery.

Walking along Leith Road he mused: "I'm going to Israel, I don't believe it!"

He thought about his previous visit to Jerusalem, and how he had poured scorn on the events of Jesus' life.

"Not now," he thought: "I'm looking forward to visiting so many places, especially Calvary where my Saviour was crucified."

He continued: "I hope Alice will be ok about my new travel arrangements!"

Babbity then shared about his experiences with Saint Margaret in Edinburgh Castle, and how she loved the scottish people. "She loves you too Babbity" replied Father John.

CHAPTER 4

Tel Aviv and beyond

When Babbity got back to the office he booked the Panorama, a 3-star hotel located on the Mount of Olives and overlooking the Dome of the Rock.

It was perfect; not too expensive and within a forty five minute walk to the centre of the Old Town and Jerusalem itself.

Going there in early springtime would ensure the weather in Israel would not be too hot!

He would leave after sorting things out with Constable Baxter and, of course, with Alice!

Alice didn't mind at all. She encouraged him to visit as many holy places as possible while he was there.

When departure day arrived he went to the café to say cheerio before ordering a taxi.

"I'm in 'wonderland' Alice," he joked as as he sat at his favourite window seat. Babbity then spoke about Saint Margaret, Alice replied, "I have feelings too!"

"Good to see you are now developing a sense of empathy and humour!" continued Alice.

"Didn't notice the change?" he replied smugly. After a good chat the taxi arrived to take Babbity to the airport.

"See you in ten days' time," said Alice. "Please pray for me."

Babbity, taking Alice in his arms and giving her a tender kiss, said: "You know I will my dear."

During the long journey Babbity felt good.

He was glad Baxter had given him all the documentation he would need for his work in Jerusalem, and after meeting Father John too, he felt ready for anything.

Looking out of the window of the plane his mind strayed again: "From the Seychelles to Israel, what a contrast! If memory serves me right the temperatures should be similar, though the Seychelles can be a little more humid. I wonder if there is anywhere that I can fish for octopus!"

"Drink Sir?" asked the air hostess.

"Yes please, give me a large whisky. I think I need it."

Babbity downed the whisky and quickly fell into a deep sleep.

After a few hours the plane prepared to land in Tel Aviv.

Of all the airports Babbity had travelled to throughout the world, Tel Aviv was his most memorable.

It was a huge circular terminal with an inverted domed ceiling, which resembled a massive upside down white saucer!

Inside the airport Babbity marvelled at the local delicacies in the various restaurants that were dotted around the periphery of this sci-fi style architectural wonder.

Babbity collected his luggage and took the yellow shuttle bus to Jerusalem, a journey of 40 minutes costing 65 shekels, about £7.

He gave the driver a bung to take him to the hotel Panorama, which was situated in an area that was fairly run down. But Babbity wasn't caring, he was in Jerusalem. That's all that mattered!

The hotel porter led Babbity to his room on the second floor. It was now 11pm and he was tired.

Before calling it a day he studied the local map he picked up at reception.

It showed the Hebron Road clearly. The road snaked its way from Jerusalem and out beyond the perimeter walls of the holy grounds.

"Ah good, at least I've got my bearings." he said.

He unpacked and was fast asleep within half an hour.

CHAPTER 5

Shaken to the core

Babbity woke about 6.30 am.

He was immediately aware of shouting and bawling. It was as though he was surrounded by an angry mob.

He sensed the crowd wanted to hurt him. Although this feeling was powerful, he also knew deep down he wasn't frightened.

Thinking the crowd were picking up heavy rocks to throw at him, he closed his eyes and looking up said: "Why are you showing me this?"

He continued muttering: "I'm not even in Jerusalem for a full day and already my mind is confused!"

"You will know soon enough!" replied a powerful external voice.

The phone rang. It was Rami, the receptionist: "Mr Babbity you have a call from Scotland!"

It was Constable Baxter: "Just to let you know Babbity the Israeli police have been in contact to alert you to new information regarding the two missing persons.

"One of them, the guy called Moshe, has a family with a bit of a reputation in Jerusalem. They must be treated with the utmost caution! They seem to have a link to an occult group in Hebron.

"We're still waiting on further information about the other person – Rachael - who seems to have been a bit of a loner. We will give you more on her background when we get it."

Baxter continued: "Babbity you still there?"

"Of course," said Babbity, "just trying to take it all in."

"Oh, nearly forgot," interrupted Baxter. "Thank you for the details you gave me from Father John; it will be most valuable. There are so many myths and theories flying around it's sometimes difficult to unravel fact from fiction.

"Anyway Babbity, enjoy your stay!" said a slightly pessimistic Baxter.

"Thanks for nothing," laughed Babbity.

He sat down on the bed, muttering: "What a start to the day!"

He put on his white casual shirt, shorts and trainers. "Time for breakfast," he mused.

The dining room was spacious and had a panoramic view from the surrounding windows. The whole of Jerusalem was bathed in early morning sunshine. There was a strong reflected light emanating from the golden Dome of the Rock.

Babbity tucked into a breakfast of cornflakes, boiled eggs, mixed fruit, couscous and pitta bread. He washed it all down with a strong coffee.

"Now for Jerusalem," he said.

This would be an exploratory day with a visit to Calvary and David's Tomb.

"I can check out the missing people in the next couple of days. Bags of time," he thought.

He strolled down the Jericho Road towards the small pathway that led to the outer perimeter wall of the old Jerusalem.

He turned right at the Dung Gate which was situated on Mac Hashalom Street.

The area was bustling with tourists, but he felt an irresistible force pull him towards the Holy Sepulchre Church which housed the ancient Holy Site of Calvary.

The journey took about an hour.

Passing through a myriad of colourful Old Town shops and bazaars Babbity's appetite began to increase because of the waft of different aromas coming from the street café's.

He also passed through the Via Dolorosa, the exact route Jesus took during the carrying of his Cross.

Babbity was emotional as he neared Calvary.

His demeanour changed to that of an excited child. He began to cry uncontrollably.

Passing through the entrance of the Holy Sepulchre Church, which was situated in a small square courtyard, he turned immediate right and made his way up the stairs to Calvary itself.

He was in luck, only a few tourists were waiting to see the place where Christ was crucified.

As he neared the exact spot, he was astounded at the icons of gold and silver that surrounded the altar.

The sense of sanctity was breathtaking.

Hundreds of burning candles brought a supernatural element to the Altar of Calvary.

Babbity fell on his knees and crawled to the spot of the Crucifixion, which was a hole in the ground under the altar.

As he pushed his hand through the hole his index finger touched the rough ground underneath, bringing his emotions to the surface.

He began to wail.

The tears just kept coming and coming; he was a physical and emotional wreck.

"Now you are here my son. You will not forget this day," Jesus said audibly. "Go therefore, and spread my Good News to everyone."

Babbity couldn't answer; he was caught up in a massive whirlwind of emotional healing.

After what seemed like ages, he finally stood up and walked to the small wooden seats that surrounded the altar.

He slumped down and began to cry again. Only this time the emotional crying was deeper. He knew it was deeper.

Thinking about all the people he had hurt throughout his life, he could only muster one word in reply: "Sorry."

Time seemed to be at a standstill. He wasn't even aware of the surrounding pilgrims. He was alone in his thoughts.

He sat there for at least two hours.

An inner strength flowed all over him, and he felt a massive emotional weight come off his shoulders.

Heaving a huge sigh of contentment, Babbity left the Holy Sepulchre Church and headed to the nearest coffee shop.

He was shaken to the core.

"Coffee sir?" asked the waiter, bringing him back to his senses.

"Yes, a latte please," he muttered.

Babbity felt elated and emotionally released; it was as if Jesus was sitting right there next to him.

Babbity thought: "I could go home right now, saying my trip was a success. If only the world at large could experience what I have just experienced. Father John will be delighted."

After finishing his coffee he made his way back to the hotel. He said to himself: "I need to take stock of all this. No more visits today. I'll make a fresh start in the morning."

CHAPTER 6

War and Peace

Babbity awoke early following a good sleep. After breakfast he headed towards the small pathway on the left hand side of Jericho Road which led to the City of Jerusalem.

Before turning off the road he noticed a church on his right hand side. It was the Church of all Nations. It was adjacent to the Garden of Gethsemane where Jesus wept tears of blood.

"Must visit there soon," he said.

Within a few minutes he had passed the Dung Gate and was heading up the hill towards David's Tomb.

"Why am I being drawn there?" he thought.

The room that housed David's Tomb was small. A dark blue silk cover was draped over the large sarcophagus.

Suddenly, he heard an audible voice: "Davidoff!"

Babbity's new found sense of humour kicked in: "Oh David's off is he!"

Again there was silence as the long trail of people filed past him.

Babbity pondered: "What on earth is happening? First, the incident yesterday morning regarding the rocks and now this word! I wish Father John was here, he would throw some light on all of this."

Prior to leaving the hotel the Israeli police phoned Babbity with addresses for the two missing persons.

He now had a mixture of emotions as he departed David's Tomb to complete his mission.

Moshe Barushkov's family lived on Malki Tsedek Street, round the corner from where he was and not far from the Hebron Road which led to the Cinematheque.

Babbity steadied himself and said: "I guess a prayer would help."

He said the Our Father which Father John had taught him.

He arrived at Moshe's front door and rang the bell.

An elderly voice shouted: "Who is it?"

Babbity responded with trepidation: "I have information about Moshe."

The front door opened gradually.

A small, plump woman in her 80s stood staring at him. She looked confused.

"Yes, what about Moshe?" she asked as she adjusted her black and white head-scarf.

Babbity said: "I have information about his disappearance. Are you his mother?"

In a frail croaking voice, the old woman cautiously answered: "Yes, I'm his mother!"

Babbity paused before saying: "It might be better if I come inside to give you my information."

She led Babbity inside her small dwelling. It was sparsely furnished with old style Artex wall plastering.

Babbity, sitting down on the worn garden feature couch, said: "How long has it been since you last heard from Moshe?"

"Oh, about 8 years ago," she said. "We held a farewell party for him as he was going to a new job in Scotland to a place called Edinburgh! But we have been worried sick since as we haven't heard of him!"

Babbity, having explained about the vaults, the bones and the DNA tests, said: "Unfortunately, Mrs Barushkov I have to tell you that your son is dead."

She began to weep and weep.

Babbity sat for a long time comforting the old woman.

After her tears dried up she said in a whisper: "At least the waiting and uncertainty is over. I will tell my husband and other children."

Babbity stood up and said his farewells, adding: "I will let the authorities know you have been informed, and we will make arrangements for the ashes to be returned."

He headed towards the main road.

On the way back to the hotel he thought: "I'm supposed to be enjoying myself. From the elation of yesterday – to this!"

"It is the Cross!" said the all-too familiar heavenly voice in response.

After his experience Babbity decided to leave his visit to the relatives of the second victim for a couple of days.

He glanced to his right at the brow of the hill and noticed a sign saying "Oscar Schindler's Grave".

"Oscar Schindler, what his grave?" he said. Babbity could hardly believe it.

"Schindler's List, I loved that film, he said. "This I gotta see!"

The wrought iron entrance gate was open, so he set about finding the grave.

Babbity well remembered the ending of the film when the people Schindler had saved from the gas chambers during the second world war appeared. Each laid a stone on his grave.

That scene came back to him when eventually he found the grave at the lower end of the cemetery.

Silently standing there for a few moments he picked up some rocks and placed them at the grave. "For mum and sister Mhairi," he said.

Then a pang of sadness entered his heart. He thought about his father who had left his mother when Babbity was a child.

"Should I?" he thought. He continued: "Och, why not!" He then placed a rock for his father too.

Babbity sat at the graveside for quite a while. He said what prayers he knew, which wasn't a lot!

After a while it dawned on him that in the past couple of days he was experiencing a whole new set of emotions.

From elation and sheer joy to emotional healing and prophecy. Now sadness, and above all forgiveness, started to creep into the normally stoic attitude of his mind set and guarded lifestyle.

He was experiencing real empathy too.

He said: "It could only happen through Jesus. This transformation, only Jesus. Praise you Jesus. Praise you Jesus."

In an instant Babbity lapsed into a form of angelic tongues.

He was aware of something happening. It felt good. He raised his voice even higher and was almost sure he could hear the Angelic Choirs accompanying him.

Babbity was in Heaven, quite literally.

His singing in tongues lasted for around 30 minutes.

"Now you will have a much closer relationship with your guardian angel," said the heavenly voice.

Suddenly he stopped singing.

He was amazed. Now he was standing outside the cemetery again!

"Wherever you are Oscar, thanks for listening," he shouted joyously.

As he moved down the hill again he felt as though he was on some sort of spiritual conveyor belt.

"I need a coffee," he said.

He stopped at a small roadside shop. He was in luck. There was a coffee machine there.

Sipping his coffee he noticed a young Israeli soldier was drinking coffee too.

The soldier approached Babbity. "How are you?" he asked.

"I'm fine," replied Babbity.

A conversation ensued about how good machine guns are!

The soldier said: "You know, when I fire a bullet it's very accurate. Not only that but when it hits the intended victim it doesn't travel in a straight line, it zig- zags through the body. This causes maximum damage!"

Babbity thought about the contrast regarding what had happened to him during the last 48 hours and the stark reality of the tensions in Jerusalem.

In a calm voice he responded to the soldier: "That's interesting, just a pity people are killed!"

"It's kill or be killed," replied the soldier, and pointing to his forehead said: "Look, look at that scar on my head. That was caused by a terrorist trying to kill me!"

Babbity asked innocently: "What happened to the attacker?"

"I shot him," said the soldier.

Babbity's stomach churned: "Lord get me away from here," he said internally.

Just at that moment the soldier was distracted. He said: "Need to go, it looks as though I'm needed at the gate. Nice to have met you."

"Same here," replied Babbity. He thought: "That was a quick reply Lord."

"When you ask me from the heart, I will always respond," said Jesus.

He stood there shaking his head, and sipping the last few dregs of coffee muttered: "What a day Lord, what a day. War and Peace indeed!"

Babbity was now experiencing two-way conversations with the Lord. He felt comfortable with the fact that Jesus was speaking to him freely.

He glanced at his watch, it was after 8pm and it was beginning to get dark. He looked up at the sky - a golden glow had spread throughout the horizon.

"Looks like good weather again tomorrow," he said happily.

CHAPTER 7

Gethsemene

Babbity awoke to the sun rising in a pool of crimson and gold spreading light all over Jerusalem.

"Gonna be a scorcher again," he said.

After breakfast he put on his favourite all-white outfit.

As he walked down Jericho Road the Church of all Nations came into view, prompting him to think: "Must visit it."

To get there he would have to pass through the Garden of Gethsemane. This meant nothing to Babbity! It was just another name in the long list of names associated with the Holy Land.

It was only 9am, but already there was a build up of pilgrims flowing through the gate.

"Must be popular," he thought.

On entering the garden he immediately sensed a serenity.

He looked at the ancient trees, but still did not make any spiritual connection.

People all around him were taking photographs which prompted Babbity to ask one of the pilgrims: "What is this place?"

A Japanese woman answered: "It's the Garden of Gethsemane. Jesus wept blood here!"

Suddenly Babbity had a mental picture of the old lady he had visited the day before. She was crying profusely for her dead son.

He heard the supernatural voice speaking again: "Suffering."

But Babbity still could not put the connection together.

As he walked around the small garden towards the church his eyes became fixed on a display board. It read: "These trees are over 2000 years old. This is were Jesus wept for the whole world before his Crucifixion. Please be silent."

Babbity exclaimed under his breath: "That's it! The old lady was weeping for her son. Jesus was weeping for us - his sons and daughters."

He fell to his knees and began to weep.

After what seemed like an eternity he wiped away the tears and headed for the Church of all Nations.

He was immediately fascinated by the multi-coloured stained glass windows on either side of the church.

Many pilgrims were blocking his view of the large main altar, so he sat at the back of the church.

The early morning sunshine was breaking through the large entrance doors and bathing the whole central isle in glorious rays of light.

From his position he could see a lot of people praying beside a large stone at the front of the altar.

Eventually, as the crowds began to dwindle, he found himself kneeling down at the small black fence around the stone.

Again it happened, Jesus spoke: "I cried here for you. I cried for the sins of the world."

Babbity just buckled with emotion, thinking: "Calvary, now this!"

As he stared at the sacred rock in front of him he was positive he saw a mental image of Jesus lying there, sweating blood.

His tears just flowed and flowed.

"Why Lord, why are you showing me this?" he asked.

"Because, I chose to," replied Jesus.

Babbity was stunned. He knelt there in a spiritual haze.

Suddenly a soft firm hand rested on his shoulder. He nearly jumped through the roof, thinking Jesus had touched him physically!

He turned around in trepidation. A familiar face was smiling down at him.

It was Benjamin, his next door neighbour from Edinburgh!

As Babbity heaved a sigh of relief he asked: "What on earth are you doing in Jerusalem? Even more so, you're in a chapel. I thought you were Jewish?"

Benjamin took Babbity by the arm and led him outside of the church where they continued their conversation.

Benjamin said: "You're asking me why I'm here! But why are you here, especially in a Catholic chapel? You're an atheist are you not?"

Babbity shrugged: "It's a long story, let's just say I've seen the light!"

Benjamin said he was a Messianic Jew.

"A Messianic Jew, what does that mean?" asked a confused Babbity.

"It means I am still following the Torah, the holy book of Judaism. But, more importantly, I truly believe Jesus is the Messiah," explained Benjamin.

"I came to know this through a Messianic group I met here in Jerusalem. They explained the full meaning of Isaiah 53, which details before, during and after Christ's Crucifixion. Do you know about that reading?"

Babbity answered: "Strangely enough I do, but why don't Jews believe your version of Isaiah 53?"

"Because they still believe the Messiah is still to come. They put a totally different slant on Isaiah 53. It's known as the Hidden Reading because there is a reluctance to discuss our take on it!"

Babbity said: "Just one reading, and that converted you to become a Messianic Jew!"

"Yip, it's as simple as that," said Benjamin. "There are many stories about Isaiah 53. I know of an American chat show host who became Messianic because of this phenomenal reading.

"The same guy tells the story about his Jewish father who converted on his death bed, knowing that Jesus Christ is truly the Messiah."

"That's fantastic," exclaimed Babbity.

"After what you have told me Benjamin I will study that reading."

What Babbity didn't mention was that a couple of weeks before coming to Jerusalem he had received an inner Locution regarding Isaiah 53.

"Father John mentioned the gift of prophecy when he spoke to me," thought Babbity. "Does that mean this is a confirmation?"

Benjamin suggested to Babbity he meet with his group.

"I'm sure it would be of interest to you," he said. "We have a deliverance team too!"

Babbity was enthusiastic. "Great," he said. "Would Thursday morning be ok? We can meet up at my hotel.

"Perfect," said Benjamin.

As the friends parted Babbity thought: "Well Lord, I can honestly say nothing is plain and simple when you are involved. What a journey! What a journey!"

CHAPTER 8

The Going gets tough

"Be Baw Babbity, Babbity……..."

An elderly woman's voice in the hotel bedroom next door shouted: "Mr Bowster, can you please keep the noise down."

Babbity said in a muffled voice: "Can't even sing when I'm happy!"

After breakfast Babbity prepared to meet the family of the second victim, Rachael Dayan.

He made his way across a bit of arid sandy ground which led to the perimeter wall around Jerusalem.

He followed the same route as he did previously, only this time he would continue over the brow of the hill and down the road towards the Cinematheque Theatre which was near the Menachim Begin Heritage Centre.

Rachael's house was in a large block of flats on Gayben hiram Street.

Babbity was apprehensive as he rang the bell. He knew there was an occult connection to the Dayan family!

The door was opened by a huge man covered in tattoos.

"Excuse me," said Babbity. "Is this the home of Rachael Dayan?"

"What if it is!" said the hulk.

Babbity got straight to the point. He said: "We have reason to believe that she is dead!"

"What do you mean….we?" asked the aggressive guy.

"I mean the police in Scotland and the Israeli police here in Jerusalem. They have matched the same DNA with bones found in a vault in Edinburgh. We know it's Rachael.

"She was last seen boarding a plane at Tel Aviv Airport about five years ago. Is this true?"

"What is it to you?" answered the hulk awkwardly.

"Well, we need to establish the truth. Was she seen boarding the plane?" replied Babbity.

"Don't be cheeky with me son," said the hulk.

"I'm only trying to get to the truth," said Babbity asking again: "Did anybody see her board the plane?"

The hulk bawled at Babbity: "Yes, I took her to the airport, she is my sister."

"Ah that's better, now were getting somewhere," exclaimed Babbity as he took the case paperwork out of his jacket.

"Can you please sign these papers to say your sister has been found and identified?" he asked.

The hulk signed the papers grudgingly and bundled the forms back into Babbity's sweating hands.

Just as he was about to leave the hulk shouted: "I know you. We are Legion and we will come after you!"

Babbity never even turned round. He was shaking all over.

He was conscious of the hulk following him as he left the complex, but he kept walking as quickly as he could.

He could hear the raging voice behind him: "I'm warning you, we will come after you."

Babbity took to running towards the area of Oscar Schindler's grave until it was safe.

"What a situation Lord," he said.

"You are mine, do not be afraid," replied Jesus.

Babbity felt anger and shouted: "It's alright for you. I'm the one experiencing the fear!"

Jesus replied instantly: "Do you think I never experienced fear? What about Gethsemene when I asked my Father to 'take away this cup'?"

Babbity felt terrible and cried out: "Did I just say that to my Saviour!"

He was all alone with his torrid thoughts and in the silence he trudged over the hill again and stopped at the coffee shop next to the Dung Gate.

He spotted the young Israeli soldier he spoke to the previous day and related his story to him.

The soldier shrugged his shoulders and said: "Welcome to the party! We get threats all the time. It's how you deal with it. My advice is to stay away from that area of Jerusalem."

After some idle chat, Babbity left the café.

As he walked down the Dorogh A Shiloakh roadway he passed the archaeological ruins of the ancient City of David on his right hand side.

"Hezekiah my King" he heard internally, but he took no notice. He was still in a daze after the threats from Rachael's brother.

When he reached the hotel he spotted Rami at reception and said:

"I was singing in my bedroom this morning and the woman next door shouted my name…Mr Bowster. I was wondering how she knew it."

Rami replied: "Ah, that lady. When she arrived the night before she signed the register, and I noticed she looked at your name and room number. I thought she was just being nosey. Is she bothering you?"

"No, of course not," replied a subdued Babbity. I was just curious."

CHAPTER 9

A name from the past

The following morning Babbity changed into his all-white shorts and T-shirt. He looked like a tennis player with the white trainers to match!

After breakfast he took the lift down to the lounge area where Benjamin was sitting sprawled out on one of the low-level recliner couches.

"Ah, Babbity, great to see you," he said. "Did you sleep well?"

"Fairly well," replied Babbity who then told Benjamin about his ordeal yesterday.

He said, still slightly shaken: "This big brute of a guy threatened to come after me, all because I asked him about his dead sister! He said that they were Legion. What does it mean?"

Benjamin looked seriously at Babbity and asked: "What was the guy's name?"

A nervous Babbity replied: "Nir Dayan."

Benjamin said he knew of the guy, adding: "They are Satanists. Many of the followers have been coming to our prayer group for deliverance!"

Babbity asked: "What does deliverance mean?"

Benjamin replied: "It means that a person who has been possessed is finally freed from the overwhelming clutches of Satan."

"Sounds familiar!" said Babbity.

"What do you mean?" asked an intrigued Benjamin.

"You asked yesterday how I came to believe. Well, it started because I was delivered too. A wonderful priest, called Father John Addington, delivered me from four powerful demons. The rest is history!"

An excited Benjamin said: "I knew it, I just knew it. That's what I meant when I said you should be doing this type of spiritual warfare. God has brought you into my path for this very reason!"

"You think so," exclaimed a still-dubious Babbity.

"Yes I think so," said Benjamin. "I wouldn't be asking you if I wasn't sure. Sometimes Hashem, sorry God, uses people who have been there and done it! It certainly looks like you have done it Babbity."

"But I'm not experienced enough," replied Babbity.

"We will teach you what to do," said Benjamin. "In fact, we will start tonight because I feel this guy Nir will be with us shortly!"

Babbity sat there in silence for a few seconds then blurted out: "Ok I'll do it, but tell me how you became involved in this deliverance thing anyway?"

Benjamin sat back on the couch and said: "On one of my numerous trips to Israel I met Aaron, a fellow Messianic Jew, who invited me to a deliverance session at his prayer group.

"Afterwards they invited me to join the team, and, as you said yourself Babbity, the rest is history!

"I think the word Davidoff is significant to you Babbity. I will pray that you get the answer to the revelation of that name.

Benjamin continued: "We can meet tonight at 7pm. Our group gathers in the Cinematheque building."

Babbity agreed and shaking Benjamin's hand the friends parted.

As he made his way to his room for an afternoon siesta Babbity noticed the elderly woman occupant of the adjacent bedroom opening her door.

Her face was familiar, but he just couldn't place it.

"Time for baw baw," he muttered.

After a pleasant nap Babbity awoke and made his way to reception where he spotted the elderly woman reading a magazine.

It was now 6.30pm so Babbity ordered a taxi. Just before it arrived he was surprised to see the woman standing with her face against the wall!

She was muttering: "Fifteen years!"

"What's that all about!" Babbity exclaimed as he left the hotel.

When he arrived at the Cinematheque he made his way to the prayer group meeting situated on the lowest level of the auditorium. The name on the door was 'Josep'.

He was greeted by Benjamin who introduced him to Aaron and the other ten team members.

Aaron smiled and studied Babbity intently. "You know what this is all about?" he asked.

"Yes, Benjamin has explained everything," said Babbity.

As everyone began to sing in tongues Babbity felt completely at home after his experience at Oscar Schindler's graveside.

He lapsed into a deep form of angelic tongues.

During it he experienced a strength and courage coming over his whole body. It was as though God Almighty had poured an elixir of supernatural protection over his now-strengthened soul.

The meeting lasted two hours and Babbity listened intently to what was said.

As everyone departed Aaron said to Babbity: "I watched you carefully tonight. You seemed at ease singing in tongues, that's important. We will wait to see if Nir makes an appearance. I fully expect him to, but we will be ready. If Hashem is for us who can be against us?"

Benjamin led Babbity upstairs to the main foyer.

"That's it my friend," he said. "You are up to speed. We just have to wait now. Nir will know we meet on a Thursday, and I fully expect him to come to try to disrupt our group."

Babbity thanked Benjamin for everything, saying: "See you on Thursday."

When Babbity arrived back at the hotel Rami at reception handed him a note from the elderly woman.

It read: "I have left the hotel but will be in Jerusalem another week if you want to call me. Here is my contact number!"

Babbity was shocked but not surprised as he had recognised her from somewhere.

"Anyway, tomorrow is another day," he said. "Time to relax."

CHAPTER 10

There is power in the name of Jesus

After breakfast Babbity had a free day, so he put on the kilt regalia he had brought with him and went for a walk. He thought: "Who was that guy called Hezekiah in my dreams last night, and who was the woman with her face to the wall?"

Suddenly an audible supernatural voice bellowed 'Come to the Sepulchre'.

Babbity was amazed. He said: "Now I know where to go today!"

Walking across the pathway, which led from Jericho Road, he glanced all around.

To his left he could see some caves cut into the orange coloured sandstone hillside. It looked like an ancient settlement or place of worship.

He noticed a camel. It's keeper was feeding it.

The scene brought back memories. He reminisced about his time in the Sudan in Northern Africa when he was 20, just after his training as an engineer had been completed.

This allowed him to travel the world with his job. With a smile on his face he thought about the time he and his work mates ended up drunk in charge of some camels - in the middle of the desert!

"What a place to put a swimming pool and bar that sold McEwans Pale Ale! Those were the days," he said.

Now five years later he was content in his new job as a travel agent.

It was now mid morning as he neared the Dung Gate.

There were throngs of tourists mulling around waiting to enter the Old Town of Jerusalem.

He glanced upwards: "Blue skies all the way," he murmured.

He stopped for a coffee and was soon aware of a tall man dressed in a black fedora-style hat, black three quarter length coat and black shoes.

The stranger approached asking where he came from.

"From Edinburgh in Scotland," replied Babbity.

"Ah Scotland, the land of the kilt," muttered the stranger as he admired Babbity's highland outfit.

Soon they were in conversation.

It turned out Moshe Davidoff was a rabbi who was on his way to the synagogue. He was also a teacher of psychology at a local college.

The talk became even more interesting when Moshe told Babbity the Hebrew word for Love

"Ahavah, I'll take a note of that," said Babbity.

During the conversation Babbity felt a surge of the Holy Spirit well-up within him, and he blurted out: "There is power in the name of Jesus!"

Moshe nearly dropped his coffee. He looked as though he was stunned at Babbity's words.

As his new-found friend indicated he was now running late for prayer time, they quickly exchanged contact details.

And in a flash, Moshe was gone.

"Wonder if I'll ever see him again?" thought Babbity.

Babbity finished his coffee and headed to the security check at the Dung Gate.

The Israeli soldiers treated him with great respect when they saw his kilt.

A young soldier said: "Ah, pure class!" as he waved him through security.

Babbity thought: "The kilt certainly opens doors!"

Babbity strode confidently towards the old town. The western wall on his right hand side was thronged with people.

"Need to go there," he muttered, "I've never been to the Wailing Wall."

As he entered the hallowed ground he put on the kippah, the rounded cap, as a sign of respect.

And as it is tradition to write down prayers and place them between the gaps in the huge stone blocks Babbity carefully placed his and began to pray.

It was an historical emotional moment for him. As he stood there with tears streaming down his face he was aware of levitating off the ground for a few seconds!

Babbity was in a sublime ecstasy.

The person standing next to him said: "I saw that. Hashem must be close to you.

He told Babbity it was reported last week that a married couple also levitated.

"It's a powerful place you know," he added.

After his experience Babbity made his way through another security point into the intriguing world of the Old Town.

He was drawing admiring glances from tourists and shop keepers as his kilt swished from side to side.

He stepped into one of the shops that had a vast array of t-shirts. Babbity settled on a red casual one with silver writing on it. It read:

"Before you try to change the world, change yourself first, that is the ultimate wisdom we should strive for"

Babbity was in Shangri-la as he left the shop, but he soon came down to earth with a "whap!"

A guy passed by carrying a wooden cross and it whacked him on the head!

Babbity realised it was a Stations of the Cross procession, and it was at the fifth station, marking Jesus' torturous journey to Calvary.

He looked at the plaque on the wall which read: "Jesus falls for the first time."

After a short prayer reflection Babbity made his way to the Holy Sepulchre.

As he stared in amazement at the ornate and ancient looking door facade and entrance way, tourists were sitting on the steps to the right of the large doors.

Babbity followed the pathway around to the left until he reached an open square, and there in the middle sat a fairly small elegant looking building.

"It is my tomb," said Jesus.

On entering the sepulchre, Babbity bowed his head in humble respect. He stood within the main chamber staring at the inner tomb area.

He entered the smaller room which contained Jesus' Sarcophagus.

Babbity sank to his knees and rested his head on top of the tomb stone.

He wept openly.

He felt another emotional release which shook his whole being to the core.

Internally, he heard a voice say: "I am not alone."

He knew it was Jesus speaking but couldn't discern what it meant. He thought: "Another question for Father John."

Walking through the exit door of the church, Babbity glanced at his watch. He couldn't believe it was 4.30pm. "Where had all the time gone?" he said.

As he walked through the streets of the Via Dolorosa he made his way to the coffee stand.

Babbity was surprised but delighted to see his friend Rabbi Moshe, who had also dropped in for a coffee.

As he approached he seemed to be in a daze, prompting Babbity to ask: "Are you ok Moshe?"

A shaken Moshe replied: "I dropped my mobile phone right there a few seconds ago, and when I bent down to pick it up there was a leaflet lying next to it.

"It said 'there is power in the name of Jesus!'"

Handing the leaflet to Babbity he said: "You said that to me today!"

Babbity was dumbstruck.

Moshe continued: "And as soon as I mentioned the word Jesus just now my heart began to feel something of a loving presence!"

Babbity answered: "I think Jesus is revealing himself to you."

Moshe indignantly said: "But I don't like Jesus!"

"Well he loves you Moshe," said Babbity. "And He is giving you a direct answer about your continued scepticism."

Moshe seemed perplexed and stayed silent.

Babbity said lovingly: "You now know that He is the Messiah!"

Moshe pointing to the leaflet said: "I'm busy telling students the Messiah is still to come, and now this is telling me Jesus is the Messiah!"

Again, when Moshe said "Jesus"a powerful surge of love swept through his heart.

He said to Babbity: "It's happening again. Jesus is touching my heart."

Moshe was searching for answers.

He turned to Babbity and asked: "What should I do?"

Babbity thought for a moment before answering: "I would tell Jesus you love Him. Tell Him you are sorry for offending Him."

A relieved Moshe said:"Is that all I do?"

"Yes, that's all you do," responded Babbity.

He looked at Babbity with pleading eyes and asked: "Can you say a prayer with me?"

Babbity had never prayed with anyone before, but he found the courage to say: "Yes, I can say a prayer with you Moshe!"

They walked to a quiet spot where Babbity prayed: "Jesus please continue to pour your healing precious blood over Moshe. Thank you Lord for revealing your powerful divinity to him, and thank you for letting him see you truly are the Messiah."

Moshe started to cry.

The very mention of "Jesus" had brought on further emotional healing.

He looked at Babbity and pleaded: "Can I meet you again?"

Babbity responded: "Of course you can. In fact, I have friends here who are Messianic Jews, and it would be good for you to meet them."

Moshe replied: "Messianic Jews? I don't understand."

Babbity explained: "It means they are still in the Jewish Faith, but accept that Jesus is the Messiah."

Moshe looked relieved and replied: "Does that mean I am Messianic?"

"It certainly looks like it Moshe," said Babbity. "What else can I say about the experience you have just received."

"But I'm a Rabbi," said Moshe.

"So was Jesus," replied Babbity confidently.

Moshe was stunned. He never expected to hear that.

Moshe rested his hand on Babbity's shoulder and said: "Thank you for your love and tenderness. I will phone you soon to arrange a meeting with your friends."

"Sounds good to me," replied Babbity.

They went their separate ways.

As Babbity headed for the hotel he thought about the conversation with Moshe.

"Me tender, me loving!" he said.

"Yes, love is all," said the inner voice.

Babbity said: "I thank you Jesus my Saviour for this experience with Moshe. It proves to me that you are Divine and your ways are true. Please continue to flow through me."

When Babbity arrived back at the hotel he made his way to his room just as the phone rang.

It was Rami at reception to inform him the mystery elderly woman was at his desk requesting to see him.

"Tell her I'll come down in a couple of minutes," said Babbity.

When he arrived she was sitting on a couch sipping an orange juice. She had an air of contentment about her.

"Babbity introduced himself and asked: "What can I do for you?"

She apologised for all the secrecy, but said she had to be sure it was him.

Inviting him to sit down she asked: "How old are you Babbity?"

Taken aback a bit he replied: "I'm 27."

"Oh, that would be about right," she said. "I want you to cast your mind back to when you would have been about 12 years old. Can you remember visiting a synagogue in Edinburgh with your sister Mhairi?"

Babbity had a good memory and he did remember.

"Do you also remember speaking to a woman about her illness?" asked the woman.

"Yes, come to think of it I do!"

"Can you remember saying a short prayer with your sister for that woman?"

Babbity paused for a few seconds and replied: "Yes I do."

The woman said: "Your sister received a prophetic word while both of you were praying with the woman, didn't she?

"Yes, I remember that too," replied Babbity.

"Can you remember what the prophecy was?"

Babbity replied: "Now you are really testing my memory. What is this some sort of inquisition?" he said.

The woman looked at Babbity lovingly and said: "Just be patient, you will soon know."

Babbity glanced at her and said: "Yes, I vaguely remember something about King Hezekiah extending the woman's life for 15 years. Is that correct?"

"Yes, that's correct Babbity," said the woman who paused, took a deep breath and with a smile on her face added: "I am that woman!"

Babbity was dumbstruck!

"Yes Babbity, it was me, and here I am 15 years later sitting in Jerusalem speaking to you!"

A puzzled Babbity asked: "But how did you know I was here?"

"Your sister Mhairi told me where you worked as a travel agent. They told me you were in Jerusalem and that you were staying at the Panorama Hotel. I decided to follow you.

"But I must tell you something else," she insisted.

But Babbity interrupted by asking her name.

"Oh, I forgot to tell you it's Ruth," she said.

Babbity responded: "Ok Ruth, what else do you have to tell me? This day has been full of surprises!"

With a loving smile she said: "I'm dying Babbity!"

Ruth paused before continuing: "It's now 15 years since that wonderful day when your sister received the prophecy from Hezekiah.

"In the Old Testament Hezekiah was also dying, so he stood up and faced the wall asking for the Lord to extend his life.

"The Lord relented and granted him an extra 15 years because of his goodness as a king.

"That's why I stood looking at the wall in the hotel reception, hoping you would make the connection!"

Babbity was overwhelmed and cried.

He couldn't believe Ruth had came all this way to to tell him this story.

"But there's more," exclaimed Ruth.

"Many years ago I was friendly with Aaron, your father."

Before she could go on Babbity interrupted again and shook his head again in disbelief.

He said: "This is developing into a complete shock to my system! My father left the family when I was young!"

Ruth continued: "That's right Babbity. Your father took a nervous breakdown and walked away from everything.

"Your mother Morag tried to find him but she never did."

A grieving Babbity asked: "Where did he go?"

"To Holland where he had friends who were members of a synagogue," replied Ruth.

"Friends in a synagogue!" said Babbity in disbelief.

Ruth took a deep breath: "Did you not know your father was Jewish? That's how we met. He would come to my synagogue in Edinburgh!"

Babbity was speechless but it began to dawn on him - about the Jewish connection.

He thought about the dreams, Hezekiah and the word Davidoff. It was all beginning to make sense.

He sat in silence for a few seconds, then said: "You know Ruth, when I was at David's Tomb I heard the name 'Davidoff'. I couldn't for the life of me think what it meant."

Ruth sat back on the couch and said: "That's your father's real name! He kept that hidden from your mother."

"What!" exclaimed an exasperated Babbity.

Ruth continued: "Your sister Mhairi knew your father didn't tell your mother mainly because she was an atheist. That's why your sister brought you to the synagogue that

day!"

Babbity's thoughts were in overdrive.

He said: "But why did God allow my father to have a breakdown? I can't understand it."

Ruth took Babbity's hand and held it tenderly. She said: "Aaron was a survivor of the concentration camps. His mind would have been fragile."

After a short while Babbity turned to Ruth and said: "So obviously you are Jewish too?"

"That's correct Babbity" she replied.

He shuffled his feet nervously and asked: "Can I assume my father is dead?"

"Yes, I'm sorry to say," replied Ruth sympathetically. "I received word of his death from his friends in Holland. I can give you their contact details.

Tears streamed down Babbity's face again. He said: "Yes, it would be good to keep in touch with them."

Babbity took Ruth's hand and asked: "And what about you? You are telling me that you are dying!"

She replied: "I'm completely at peace with that Babbity. I've still got a few months to enjoy what God has given me.

"I've had a good long life. I'm now 86 years old and waiting for the great day when I meet Hashem face to face."

Babbity was in tears again. Ruth put a frail consoling arm around his broad shoulders and said: "Babbity, we all have to die one day. I will wait for you in Heaven."

Babbity stared at Ruth lovingly, exclaiming: "But you're so calm!"

"It's the Holy Spirit," she replied. "He takes care of me the way Hezekiah did all those years ago."

Babbity was so taken with Ruth he asked if he could meet up with her in Edinburgh after he returned.

"Of course you can Babbity," she said. "I leave tomorrow so I've booked a hotel nearer to the airport.

"Good thinking," remarked Babbity.

Ruth said: "I'm so glad I managed to make contact with you again. It was imperative that I did so."

She reached into her handbag and gave her card to Babbity. It read: Ruth Goldberg, Archaeologist, Princess Street Gardens, Edinburgh.

Ruth stood up unsteadily. She was painfully gaunt. Babbity could see her shoulder bones poking through her thin white blouse.

Babbity ordered her a taxi.

She left smiling. Her small frame camouflaged a wonderful strength of spirit and determination.

The whole day had left Babbity physically drained.

CHAPTER 11

The dark side

He awoke late in the morning. It was Wednesday and he was meeting Benjamin and his team.

He strolled around the city again taking in all the splendour and contemplating on everything that happened the day before.

In the afternoon he phoned Benjamin and then made his way to the Cinematheque Conference Centre.

When he arrived Benjamin greeted him. Babbity couldn't wait to tell him about his experience with Ruth.

He added: "She filled in a lot of the missing links in my life. I feel so much more at peace now."

"Great Babbity," said Benjamin. "This seems to be a very enlightening time for you."

On a more serious note he said: "We now have to prepare our strategy regarding Nir. I expect him to try to disrupt our prayer group. He will know that we meet here every Wednesday at 3 pm."

"How come he knows that?" enquired Babbity.

Benjamin said: "Because his dead sister Rachael came here occasionally. She was Messianic."

Babbity said: "If it happens, then so be it."

"Good Babbity," replied Benjamin. "After all, you had some training and advice a couple of days ago from Aaron that will give you confidence."

Approaching the prayer group hall, melodic tongues filled the air.

Before they went in Babbity's mind strayed back to the vaults in Edinburgh and the demon Gash.

He realised Gash would have sensed Rachael was Messianic. This would have given the demon added satisfaction.

Breaking his thought pattern, Aaron said: "Welcome Babbity. Come over here, we will pray over you."

In an instant, Babbity surrendered his heart mind soul and body to Jesus.

He felt an overwhelming sense of peace and joy flow through him. He could hear someone prophesying: "You will become a warrior for Jesus Christ. You will travel in his name and you will be his witness, casting out demons!"

Babbity fell to his knees and rested in the Holy Spirit.

After a few moments Aaron asked for silence. "Let the Holy Spirit speak to us again," he whispered as they made their way to the seats.

Then a voice from the group broke the silence. It was Jesus speaking: "No matter what happens I am in control of the situation. Remember, I have conquered the world."

Suddenly a howling voice could be heard from the back of the hall. The scream pierced the silence.

The mocking voice bawled: "The meek shall inherit the earth, ha ha ha."

It was Nir. He stood there in an all-conquering pose, flexing his massive muscles.

Then he strode to the front of the hall and screamed at Aaron: "I am Hell Fire and you will be my servant!"

Aaron was calm, having seen it all before. He replied to the demon inside Nir: "I am the servant of Jesus Christ."

Nir went crazy. He screamed: "I hate him. I hate him."

Two male members of the deliverance team grabbed hold of Nir. They were every bit as big as him, standing at six feet five and with muscles to match!

Nir tried to free himself, but the spiritual minders only increased their hold on him.

Aaron looked straight into the red eyes of Nir and said calmly: "Who are you?"

There was no response. Nir just laughed.

Aaron asked again: "In the name of Jesus of Nazareth son of the living God, who are you?"

Nir screamed: "I am Beelzebub."

A horrible shrill voice came out of Nir's foul-smelling mouth as he growled: "I will never come out of him, he's mine. I taught him to hate Rachael. She couldn't understand this, but it was me all along."

Aaron said in a commanding voice: "You will come out this time Beelzebub."

"Never, never," screamed Nir.

A member of the group splashed Holy Water over Nir. He went berserk again and fell to the floor slithering about like a snake.

"Aaron said: "Many times we have prayed with you, but this time you will come out. Do you hear me Beelzebub?"

Nir's resistance seemed to be weakening.

Aaron stood over him, and shouted in a controlled and authoritative voice: "In the name of Jesus Christ son of the living God, come out of him."

The group responded in unison: "Fire, fire, fire of the Holy Spirit. Out, out, out."

A whooshing sound like a controlled exhalation came out of Nir's mouth. It was the sign the group had been waiting for.

Nir slumped to the floor and lay motionless. The demon was gone!

Nir opened his eyes and began to smile. He stood up and said: "It's gone, its gone!"

Aaron put his arms around him and said: "Welcome home Nir!"

Babbity and the group danced around the hall in delight shouting: "Praise God, praise God."

Babbity heard internally: "Remember what you have seen here this day. I have conquered the world."

The deliverance session had lasted two hours.

Aaron turned to Benjamin and said: "Nir will now be free to live a more spiritual life."

Looking at Babbity he added: "You will be a great help to the Messiah now that you have witnessed this deliverance today.

"God has big plans for you, Babbity. You will be involved in the deliverance ministry too. And you will return to Jerusalem."

Babbity shuffled his feet nervously, replying: "If I can help Yeshua then I will."

Aaron gave Babbity a big hug before leaving the auditorium.

When he had gone Babbity asked Benjamin: "How does Aaron know that I will come back to Jerusalem?"

"The Holy Spirit will bring you back," replied Benjamin. The Good Lord needs you here."

Babbity smiled. "If you say so," he said.

Before departing they exchanged contact details with Babbity reminding Benjamin of the rabbi he spoke about.

"I'm sure he will be interested to meet your group," he said.

"Of course Babbity, said Benjamin. "Isn't Yeshua amazing!"

"He sure is," answered Babbity.

Babbity said his farewells to the rest of the group then made his way back to the hotel to pack.

It was time to go home.

VOLUME 4

(Babbity Bowster and the Dutch Connection)

CHAPTER 1

Rising

Babbity was keen to see Father John as soon as possible after returning from the Holy Land.

Father John was totally amazed at what Babbity was telling him about his experiences in Israel.

They were in the priest's small office just adjacent to the church.

Suddenly Father John stood up and said: "I knew it. Those words about Isaiah 53! I just knew instinctively that your family background was Jewish.

"I had an inclination when your sister Mhairi visited me as she seemed to be hiding something, not in a bad way of course. But she obviously had her reasons for not revealing her background.

"But getting back to Jerusalem. Are you surprised Babbity about all these revelations and spiritual experiences?"

Babbity responded: "Surprised isn't the word, more like shocked to the core!"

After a few seconds silence, he revealed he had had another supernatural dream.

"But this one was different," he said.

A curious Father John asked him to explain.

"I awoke about 3am and realised my body was rising off the bed, said Babbity. "I was horizontal and moving upwards ever so slowly.

"I could feel it physically, but I also sensed it was a supernatural experience too.

"I was at least six feet off the bed. I truly thought God was taking me to Heaven!"

Babbity continued: "After a few seconds I gradually descended until I was back on my bed again. The whole experience must have lasted about a minute."

Father John was intrigued and asked Babbity: "Can you remember doing anything unusual before you went to bed that night?"

Babbity replied confidently: "Yes, I do. I was reading the life story of St Catherine of Sienna when I heard her voice inside of me thanking me for doing so!"

Father John said a prayer over Babbity, who immediately felt a wonderful peace overcome him which seeped into his very soul.

"That's interesting Babbity, said Father John. "I was just saying a prayer to make sure."

"Make sure about what?" asked Babbity.

Father John replied: "That your experience came from the Holy Spirit. The prayer I said over you told me that it was authentic."

Babbity sat in silence before asking: "What caused the levitation?"

Father John answered: "I think St Catherine interceded for you."

Babbity quizzed: "Interceded?"

"Yes, Babbity interceded," said Father John. "St Catherine prayed for you to God the Father, and He rewarded her prayer by allowing the levitation experience. It was to let you know you will be close to the Communion of Saints.

"I would advise you to pray to the saints."

A bemused Babbity replied: "But I'm not Catholic! How can this be happening?"

Father John explained: "The word Catholic means universal. It doesn't matter if you are a Catholic or not. It seems as though God has taken a liking to you Babbity."

He started to laugh. "Get used to it. There are stalwarts of the church who would give their right arm to experience what God is lavishing on you.

"Enjoy it Babbity. It's free! God loves you and He's sharing His tender love with you.

"I also think the levitation was symbolic of God the Father, drawing you closer to Him in Heaven. Hence the rising upwards."

The enormity of what Father John had just told him was now beginning to sink in.

Stunned, and in tears Babbity shook his head in amazement.

"Thank you Father John for bringing light to all of this," he said.

"I must now begin to think about my direction of faith. I will pray to the saints to guide me!"

"That's my boy. You're learning already," laughed Father John.

A refreshed Babbity had one final question.

He said: "When I was inside the Holy Sepulchre Church in Jerusalem, I heard an interior voice say, very quietly, 'I am not alone'. What do you think that means?"

Father John responded: "It tells me Jesus was pleased you had made the effort to come to Him in Jerusalem. He certainly was not alone, knowing that you were with Him Babbity."

Father John continued: "My supper will be ready soon Babbity. So, once again I'm glad to be part of your faith journey and I look forward to the next episode."

At that they said their goodbyes.

CHAPTER 2

Ida Peerdeman

After visting the Mad Hatters Cafe to see Alice, Babbity strolled into a bookstore on Princess Street and puchased "The Mother of all Nations", a book that caught his eye.

The book described the experiences of a woman in Holland who purportedly had seen the Mother of Jesus. Her name was Ida Peerdeman.

Delighted with his purchase Babbity made his way back to the café where Alice brought him another coffee.

She joked: "Oh, back to see me again are you?"

Babbity showed her the book, and turning over the pages he said: "Look, Ida Peerdeman comes from Holland!"

"So!" inquired Alice.

"Remember I told you my father's friends came from Holland. Well, don't you think it's coincidental that this book jumped out at me?

Alice said: "Maybe you're meant to go there!"

"Never thought about it that way!" remarked Babbity.

"Well I think you should," replied Alice.

Babbity sat in the cafe for the rest of the day reading the book. He just couldn't put it down.

At closing time Alice shouted: "Well my dear, we need to lock up. Out you go!"

Babbity walked over to her and in full view of everyone planted a long and tender kiss on her lips.

Alice rested her head on his shoulders. "I love you," she said.

"I love you too my dear," said Babbity and walked out the door whistling.

He was now in Princess Street, not far from his flat. He thought maybe the Mother of Jesus has brought this book into my hands!

"Mother of Jesus," he said. "What's that all about?"

Just then he heard a female voice come into his heart. It was tender and loving and said: *"I will bring you closer to my son!"*

Babbity was stunned. "Is this the voice of Jesus' Mother?" he thought.

Internally he heard: *"Yes!"*

When he reached his flat, he slumped down onto the couch and wondered what it could all mean.

"First of all Jesus speaks to me. Now His mother is speaking to me too! It's a bit frightening!" he thought.

"Don't be frightened – accept!" replied the Mother of Jesus.

Babbity sat in silence. He thought about the glorious events in Jerusalem. Now he was on the verge of going to Holland.

"Only God could arrange all this," he said.

CHAPTER 3

More missing people

After breakfast Babbity put on his uniform and body armour.

"Time to meet constable Baxter," he said.

Within ten minutes he was at the police station.

He parked his small Fiat car outside the offices and strode confidently into Baxter's office.

"Coffee Babbity?" asked Baxter.

"Nope, had too much already," he answered.

"Ok," said Baxter. "So let's get down to work again! Where would you like to go next?"

Babbity replied: "I know Holland was mentioned at the Vaults after that carry on with Gash."

Baxter interrupted: "Ah, yes, Holland is on our list of countries of more missing people."

"Well I would like to go there," said Babbity. My late father has friends there too, and there's a certain lady I would like to visit!"

Baxter joked: "I hope Alice knows about that!"

"Oh she knows about it all right. In fact, she encouraged me to go," laughed Babbity.

"All I need to do is get more time off work, but that should be ok. They know I like to travel."

Babbity walked to the door saying: "I will let you know when I am ready to go."

Baxter replied: "That's fine. It will give us a chance to get your file names and addresses together."

After leaving the police station Babbity decided to visit Ruth Goldberg, the elderly lady he met in Jerusalem.

He phoned her that night and set up a meeting at her apartment for the next day.

After breakfast, Babbity made his way along Chapel Wynd, just beyond East Princess Street Gardens, towards Ruth's Castle View apartment.

He pushed the bell ringer.

After fumbling about for a couple of minutes Ruth finally opened the door to her brightly decorated house.

She greeted Babbity warmly with a loving embrace.

Babbity studied the various photographs of ancient artifacts on the living room walls.

As he continued to stare, Ruth said: "Interesting, eh."

"Certainly is," replied Babbity. "But I've just remembered you are an archaeologist."

"Yes," replied Ruth as she sat down and rested her weary legs.

Babbity told Ruth he was going to Holland and would visit the friends of his father that she had told him about in Jerusalem.

Ruth stumbled over to a cabinet and brought out a notebook.

She gave him two addresses, one in Apeldoorn, about 90 minutes from Amsterdam Airport, and the other in Amsterdam itself, on Diepenbrockstraat, near the Rai Conference Centre.

Babbity thanked Ruth and said: "This is an important time for me. It will help me find out what kind of man my father really was."

Ruth responded: "It's not easy going back into the past. It's like archaeology, sometimes you find what␣␣␣ your're looking for and sometimes you don't. I will pray for you."

When Babbity enquired about Ruth's health she said: "The cancer makes me feel very tired. It's a struggle sometimes getting up the stairs, but I'll be fine.

"You go and enjoy yourself. Look on it as an adventure. I always did. Be sure to let me know how you get on"

Babbity gave Ruth a loving hug before departing.

CHAPTER 4

Preparation time

When he got back to the travel agency he booked his flight to Holland for the following day.

He also got a phone call from Father John who said: "I have some important information to share with you which I should have given you at our last meeting.

"I know you have been on a high lately with all that the Holy Spirit is showing you, but, unfortunately, sometimes we have to come down off the mountain again, get our feet back on the ground so to speak."

Father John paused and then added: "Within our hearts we sometimes discern a struggle, an interior conflict between the good we want to do and a certain leaning towards sin, darkness, self righteousness and self justification.

"The second Vatican Council said ….' *for when people look into their own hearts they find they are sometimes drawn towards what is wrong and are sunk in many evils which cannot have come from their good Creator*'".

Babbity was so grateful to Father John for his words of wisdom. He thanked him for his concern and asked for prayers during his stay in Holland.

He then went to see Constable Baxter for the details of the missing persons.

"I've put your file together," said Baxter. We have another two missing persons for you. Both live in Diepenbrockstraat.

"They are Ruben Willems, aged 22, tall with dark hair and blue eyes. He went missing about 10 years ago, according to the Dutch Police.

"The other is Lucas Janssen, about 6ft, slim built with brown eyes. He was only 18 years old when he went missing five years ago.

Babbity said: "That Gash has a lot to answer for."

After discussing other details about the missing persons, Constable Baxter wished Babbity a rewarding and safe trip.

That evening Babbity and Alice went for a Chinese meal on Rose Street.

"Well my dear, that's me off on my travels again," said Babbity as he stuffed a forkful of noodles into his mouth.

Alice said: "I think these trips are meant to happen. Your spiritual journey has been remarkable. Just to think it all started when I met you at the Carnival Fair in Princess Street!"

Babbity joked: "Yea, and I even won you a pink elephant. Hope you've still got it!"

"Of course I have," she replied.

They spent the next couple of hours together, laughing and joking.

CHAPTER 5

Amsterdam

A shot rang out, then another. Two concentration camp prisoners lay dead.

The shots came from a telescopic rifle held by the camp commandant.

The other prisoners could only look on in subdued horror as the marksman casually took aim again.

"Landing time sir, fasten your seat belt," said the air hostess, bringing Babbity's film thoughts about Schindler's List abruptly to a close.

Schippol Airport was like a small town within a town. It had plenty of shops in the main concourse and was always busy.

Babbity noticed wooden daffodils in one of the shops. He would get some for Alice on the return journey.

He booked a train to the Rai Conference Centre, which was a stones' throw from the Apollo Hotel where he would be staying.

The hotel was modern with a huge glass frontage. It sat next to a canal which flowed directly through the Diepenbrockstraat.

Babbity threw his case down and flopped onto the bed.

He decided to go to the missing persons' families tomorrow, giving him more time to find his father's friends in Apeldoorn.

He slept well that night.

BABBITY BOWSTER AND THE CHOCOLATE TEARDROPS

After breakfast he made his way to the first address that Constable Baxter had sourced.

On the way he noticed a small chapel with a picture on the front door. The name above it said the Lady of all Nations.

"I don't believe it," he spoke. "That's similar to the title of the book I read before coming here – the Mother of all Nations.

He decided to visit the chapel.

As he crossed the road he had a mental picture of an old woman with short dark hair. She was wearing a green coat. Then he heard internally "Ida".

The chapel was empty. On the wall to the left of the main altar was a large picture of a lady standing in front of a black cross. She was all in white and standing on a globe of the world with sheep at her feet.

Three rays were coming from each hand. She had a golden sash around her waist and was wearing a short golden mantle around her long dark curly hair.

The lady looked as though she was only 18 years old and she looked Jewish.

Babbity fell on his knees. He heard an audible voice: *"Welcome, my son. I have led you here."*

Babbity was at ease as he knelt there, lost in time.

He heard another internal voice: *"Come back again before you leave."*

As he left the chapel he came across a leaflet giving a history of the apparitions.

"Will check this later," he thought.

The internal words Babbity was hearing came so natural. It was as though his own mother was speaking.

He made his way along Diepenbrockstraat.

Most of the apartments were in two and three level blocks. On the opposite side was Beatrix Park which was behind the chapel.

There was a few cafes at the far end of Diepenbrockstraat so he popped in for a coffee.

His mind shot back to his first visit to Amsterdam when he was leading a fairly hedonistic lifestyle. He was only 19 years old and his stark memory was the red light district.

How things had changed he thought.

Babbity's first visit would be to the Lucas Janssen family who lived just 50 yards along the street.

He said a short prayer before ringing the bell.

As he waited for the door to open he heard an audible voice again. It was the same Lady who spoke to him in the chapel: *"I want to be known and loved by all."*

An old man appeared.

He was short in height and frail.

"Excuse me," said Babbity, is this the Janssen household?"

The old man acknowledged that it was.

"I'm a special constable from Scotland," said Babbity, "and we have reason to believe Lucas Janssen lived here up until he was about 13 years old."

"Come in," said the old man who made his way to the kitchenette to put on the kettle.

"What do you want to know?" he asked.

Babbity replied: "It's not what I want to know it's what I have to tell you."

The old man poured out two teas and sat down next to Babbity at the kitchen table.

Babbity continued: "We have reason to believe the DNA of bones found in Scotland match perfectly to that of Lucas Janssen. Are you related to him?"

The old man looked agitated and nervously sipped his tea.

He said: "Lucas was my adopted son. He came from a family of Jewish immigrants. I adopted him after his mother and father split up. It was all to do with drugs.

"Both parents were vagrants. Lucas never stood a chance, so I took him into my life because I lived alone after my wife died."

The old man looked at Babbity with tears in his eyes. He continued: "We had a massive argument one day. I suspected he was drifting into the drug scene.

"I couldn't help myself. I threw him out. He was forever coming in late and always seemed to be intoxicated or out of his head with drugs.

"I just flipped. I never told anybody he was gone, but, to my eternal shame, I never did look for him.

"I was just relieved to be free of the misery. I know it sounds selfish, but I just couldn't handle it anymore."

Babbity took another sip of tea. He remembered when he visited Amsterdam as a teenager and how easy it was to get caught up in drugs.

Babbity asked the old man: "Did you know the name of Lucas's parents?"

In a croaking voice the old man replied: "Yes, the father's surname was Davidoff!"

Babbity gulped asking: "Are you sure it was Davidoff?"

"Of course I am," replied the insistent pensioner. "I might be in my 90's but I still have a sharp mind!"

Babbity was shaken. He stayed silent with his thoughts. "Surely not!" he asked himself.

The old man looked at Babbity in surprise and asked him if he was alright.

"Yea, I'm fine," he said.

He presented ID police forms and asked the old man to sign them as proof of a positive identification of the missing Lucas.

Babbity asked the old man his name.

He replied: "I was named after my father Joseph Starsky."

Babbity said: "Well Joseph, my heart goes out to you. You must have been through many sleepless nights anxious about Lucas' whereabouts."

Joseph replied: "Yes I did, but I'm wondering what made him pick Scotland? I guess I will never know!"

Babbity stood up and shook Joseph's hand. He said: "At least there is closure on this whole tragic episode of your life."

Joseph started to cry, whispering: "It's not nice to know he is dead, but at least I know he's at peace. Well, I hope he's at peace."

"I never really had a faith, although my family were Protestant. I always felt there was something out there, but I just couldn't put my finger on it."

Babbity said: "Joseph, there is a small chapel along the road from you called the Lady of all Nations. Go there and ask her to help you."

"Her!" queried Joseph.

"Yes Her!" replied Babbity "She is a special Lady who is the Mother of Jesus and of all the children from different faiths. That's why they call her 'the Lady'. Ask her to help you."

Joseph looked at Babbity with tears streaming down his face and said: "You know I never knew my own mother. Maybe this Lady can help me."

Without hesitation Babbity exclaimed: "Exactly."

Again he heard the audible voice repeat: *"I want to be known and loved by all."*

As Babbity was about to leave Joseph said: "Take care my friend."

CHAPTER 6

Disclosure

The following morning Babbity travelled by train to Apeldoorn to find his father's friends.

The journey was just over one hour, passing factory areas until the green forested area of Appeldoorn came into view.

Babbity booked into the Hotel Fletcher, which was owned by friends of his father!

As it was still early morning he decided to have breakfast.

Babbity looked at the menu. "Think I'll go for the scrambled eggs and toast," he muttered.

Afterwards he made his way to reception to speak to the owner.

"You're speaking to him," was the friendly reply from a tall elderly man who said: "I'm Hugo."

Babbity responded: "Well, I'm Babbity Bowster from Scotland. My friend Ruth Goldberg told me you knew Aaron Davidoff, my father."

Hugo slumped into the reception chair!

Looking at Babbity he shook his head and scratched his long white curly hair.

"You're his son?" gasped Hugo. "And you know Ruth too! I think we both need to sit down."

He continued: "Would you like a drink Babbity?"

"It's a bit early," said Babbity, "but since you've offered then why not."

They went into the lounge where a roaring log fire was burning away.

"What would you like to drink," said Hugo.

"I have a feeling I will need a strong brandy," answered Babbity.

"I'll have the same," said Hugo.

As Babbity swirled the ice round in his brandy glass he looked at Hugo and said: "You looked shocked when I revealed the information about my father."

Hugo took a deep gulp of the brandy. He replied: "He always spoke about his son, but we discounted it because his mind was going.

"He always spoke about me?" asked Babbity as the tears started to flow.

Hugo took another big gulp of brandy, exclaiming: "He continually spoke about you. He could never remember anything about his marriage, but he would always speak about you."

They had another brandy.

"What did he look like, and what type of man was he? asked Babbitty.

Hugo said: "He was tall, just like you. He had dark hair, just like you, and he was well built, just like you!"

Babbity looked at Hugo with a surprised expression.

"That's the other bit I was coming too", said Hugo. "I'm his brother so you are now sharing a brandy with your uncle!"

"Another?" asked Hugo.

"Yes, make it a double!"

Babbity stretched out his hand and said:

"Uncle Hugo, it's a pleasure to meet you."

"And the same here Babbity," replied Hugo.

He continued: "Now getting back to your father. You asked what type of man he was.

"All I can say is if you look at me you see your father, physically, but our natures were completely different.

"I am an impatient person, but your father always had time for people. He would help anyone who asked him.

In fact, he was too sensitive for the world. Although his mind started to waver, he had very lucid moments talking about his time in the death camp."

"Death camp!" uttered Babbity.

Hugo took another sip of his brandy. "Yes, Auschwitz," he said.

Hugo looked at Babbity with a stern expression.

"Have you not heard of Auschwitz?" he asked.

"I've heard of it," said Babbity, "but it never meant anything to me. Until now! What did he tell you about Auschwitz."

"Do you really want to know Babbity?" asked Hugo.

Babbity replied: "I think it would help me to understand my father better."

"That's very caring of you," said Hugo. "It would also let you see why your father started to go out of his mind."

Hugo took a deep breath, and another brandy!

"One of the most peculiar things your father shared about Auschwitz was the fact that even the wildlife sensed death there.

"After the war finished no birds could be seen around the horrible camp for years!

"Your father spoke about the horrors of Auschwitz, how they had to share toilets with hundreds of prisoners, dysentery and all sorts of diseases were rife.

"There was always a fight to try to get the top bunk, for if you were in the bottom you were exposed to the human excrement from above.

"The Germans forced prisoners to stand in their pyjamas at a roll call in the middle of winter. Just imagine that, standing there in your bare feet. Some would just drop dead, frozen to death.

"Executions were commom place. The 'Standing Torture' was a concrete box with a lid on it. Prisoners set for punishment would be forced inside.

"There wasn't enough room to stand up or sit down. They were left to die in a cramped position.

"Everybody knew about the incessant murder in the gas ovens.

"Your father spoke about the flames and the constant ash falling from the sky.

"He said one of his worst experiences was being forced to take the bodies out of the gas chambers.

"They were piled in a triangular shape. It was obvious to your father that the strongest in the chamber would try to crawl to the top for any last gasp of air that was available."

Hugo let out a big sigh. He continued: "I think that was the most horrible experience for your father, dragging the bodies out of the chamber to be burnt in the coke ovens."

Babbity grabbed Hugo by the arm and said: "I think I've heard enough!"

The tears were streeming down his face. Hugo wept too.

As the night wore on, with the contents of the brandy bottle dwindling, Hugo reminisced about all the family experiences, good and bad.

The excess alcohol and traumatic stories took its toll, and both staggered off to their rooms.

CHAPTER 7
A new dawn

Babbity awoke bleary eyed.

Hugo was already working at the reception desk.

After a delicate breakfast of toast and orange juice Babbity made his way to reception.

"How's the head," asked Babbity.

"I'm fine, how are you?" asked Hugo.

"Yea, ok," replied Babbity who was still munching on his toast.

He asked: "How come everyone in Holland can speak good English?"

"Because they are taught it in school," replied Hugo.

"It just encourages my laziness, knowing I don't have to learn Dutch!" said Babbity.

He continued: "I meant to ask how you got to know my friend Ruth?"

Hugo replied: "Many years ago she came to Apeldoorn on one of her architectural expeditions. She stayed at the hotel, and I struck up a friendship with her. She has kept in touch ever since."

Babbity asked:"Did she know you and dad were brothers?"

"Of course, but she obviously wanted you to find out yourself," answered Hugo.

Babbity changed the subject.

He said: "When I was in Amsterdam yesterday I met a man who had adopted a boy called Lucas Janssen who was murdered in Scotland. I'm here to tie up the loose ends for a police enquiry back home."

Hugo asked: "Who were his parents?"

Babbity said: "Strangely enough, the surname of Lucas's parents was the same as yours Davidoff!"

Hugo looked surprised and said: "We had another Davidoff brother who was considered to be the black sheep of the family.

"He left home as a youth and nobody ever heard from him again. I was told he may have lived in the area of Diepenbrockstraat, but I never knew for certain."

"What was his first name?" asked Babbity.

"Vincent," replied Hugo.

Babbity looked at Hugo with a searching expression and asked: "Surely Vincent wasn't your long lost brother?"

Hugo glanced at the roaring fire and asked: "But how come the boy was called Janssen and not Davidoff?"

"Good question," replied Babbity. He continued: "But it will come to light eventually."

Hugo remarked: "It's interesting that Lucas ended up in Scotland. Maybe he was searching for someone?"

Babbity stood up and stretched out his arms saying: "I think I'll go for a walk to clear my head."

"Good idea." said Hugo: "All this information is starting to clog up my brain a little too. See you in a while."

Babbity strolled out through reception and was soon walking through the glorious countryside of Apeldoorn.

He marvelled at the flatness of the surrounding fields and forests. He muttered: "No wonder Hitler and his cronies made short work of Holland."

He looked into the distance along the hedge rows and couldn't believe his eyes. Coming straight towards him was a massive German Tiger tank, camouflaged as if ready for battle.

Babbity stopped to rub his eyes. "Yes, it is real," he said.

He heard Father John's voice echoing in his mind: *"Remember to come down off the mountain again!"*

The tank came closer and closer until it ground to a halt about fifty yards from Babbity's quivering body.

The turret swivelled round until it pointed directly at Babbity.

Suddenly, "whoosh," a tank shell came pounding towards him at enormous speed.

He fell onto the ground and covered his head. The shell struck a farm house directly behind him, blowing it to smithereens!

Babbity got up and ran back to the safety of the hotel.

As he entered he screamed in anguish: "Help, help."

Hugo came running towards him.

"Are you ok," he asked.

Babbity started to tremble and blurted out: "I saw a tank, a German tank!"

Hugo grabbed Babbity. "Calm down," he said: "There's no tank here. You're having a daylight nightmare! It must have been the combination of drink and the stories about Auschwitz!"

Babbity hung on to Hugo and said: "I think I need a strong coffee."

Afterwards he went for a nap. He woke up thinking: "I definitely need to cut down on the brandies!"

In the evening they met again and Hugo gave Babbity a bit of a history lesson.

He said "The city of Apeldoorn was one of the first allied objectives in the advance towards the North Sea.

"On April 16 1945, the 1st Canadian Infantry Brigade arrived. By mid morning the Highlanders had secured the North Western section of the city!"

Babbity interupted and laughed as he said: "Highlanders! I knew it. Us guys get everywhere!"

Hugo continued: "From April 11 to the 17 the Canadians suffered 506 casualties. There was very little damage to the town as the liberating allies were aware many refugees were staying here.

"Afterwards there were parades by veterans commemorating the liberation. It was a joyous occasion."

Babbity thanked Hugo for the information and said he would be leaving tomorrow.

Next day Babbity arrived early for breakfast with his bags packed. He felt much better after having a good night's sleep.

Babbity proceeded to demolish the full Scottish breakfast Hugo had specially prepared for him.

"Where did you get the square sausage?" he asked

Hugo replied: "I have my contacts everywhere!"

"Those scrambled eggs and grilled bacon were absolutely tops," beamed Babbity.

Agreeing, Hugo said: "Please tell Ruth I was asking after her. I have great memories. She is a wonderful person."

They said their goodbys and Babbity left in a sombre mood.

CHAPTER 8

The Crickles of Cricklewood

Babbity reminisced as he made his way by train to Schippol: "I've got the crickle, my mother Morag used to say."

His knees were painful, but he couldn't remember any long walks or sudden exercise.

"What about the fall in Apeldoorn!" said the Holy Spirit.

Babbity's mind couldn't take in what he was hearing.

"Surely the fall didn't damage my knees, or did it?" he questioned.

"Look at the word fall again!" repeated the Holy Spirit.

"Fall?" Babbity queried.

"Yes, fall, if it can happen to Jesus it can happen to you!"

"Did Jesus fall?" Babbity asked himself.

A few moments passed as he stared out of the window

"Yes, He fell three times on the road to Calvary," said the Holy Spirit.

"What's that got to do with me falling in Apeldoorn?" queried Babbity.

"We all have to carry our cross. That's why Jesus fell. He couldn't sustain the weight of the cross."

In deep thought Babbity paused before asking himself: "So there's hope for me. If it happened to Jesus, then we should expect a fall?"

A few more seconds passed as Babbity watched the countryside of Apeldoorn disappear into the distance.

"Everyone should expect a fall. Just ask Father John!" said the Holy Spirit.

Babbity thought back to the conversation he had with the priest before leaving for Holland: "Sometimes you have to come down off the mountain again and keep your feet on the ground, so to speak!"

Babbity wondered: "Did Father John know I would take a physical tumble or a spiritual tumble?"

"*Both!*" was the reply from the Holy Spirit.

Babbity was getting angry. "Oh, get lost!" he screamed at the top of his voice.

A few moments later came the incisive reply: *"It's not me that's lost!"*

Babbity's mind was troubled as he left the train at Schippol. He didn't seem to notice anything. The whole world just passed him by.

Leaving the station, Babbity walked by Beatrix Park and headed towards the Lady of All Nations Chapel on Diepenbrockstraat.

He heard the beautiful voice of a Lady: *"Send now your Spirit."*

"What!" he exclaimed.

The voice repeated, even more insistently: *"Send now your Spirit"*

As he entered the church Babbity noticed six woman dressed in white garments sitting at the back.

They started to recite a powerful prayer together: "Lord Jesus Christ Son of the Father, *send now your spirit* over the earth. Let the Holy Spirit live in the hearts of All Nations that they may be preserved from degeneration, disaster and war. May the Lady of All Nations, the Blessed Virgin Mary, be our Advocate."

Babbity was taken aback.

"That's the words I heard outside the chapel, *Send Now Your Spirit*," he said.

The same tender voice spoke again: *"My Son is sending His Spirit upon the earth. He is sending His Spirit into your heart Babbity."*

In the silence Babbity noticed the Lady in the large picture on the wall moving her hands!

He rubbed his eyes, but the hand movement continued.

"Grace, Redemption and Peace," he heard internally.

Babbity moved closer to the picture and saw three rays coming from each hand.

As he contemplated the meaning he noticed the six ladies leaving the chapel, realising they were all dressed the same as the Lady in the picture.

"Ah, they must be nuns," he thought.

Babbity sat in a pew in the soothing silence, gathering his thoughts.

He eventually glanced at his watch. It was 4.30pm.

He said: "Almost ninety minutes have passed and it just seems like moments."

As he was about to leave the church, he heard another interior word: *"Deliver."*

Babbity scratched his head: "Deliver, deliver what?" he thought.

"I will lead you....Deliverance!" was the reply.

Babbity remembered the last time he heard the word Deliverance was in Jerusalem when Aaron and Ben had introduced him to the Deliverance Ministry.

He then thought about Nir who was Delivered from evil spirits that day.

Babbity left the Chapel of All Nations feeling refreshed and re energised.

"What a day," he said. "Crickles of Cricklewood right enough!"

CHAPTER 9

All hell breaks loose

The early morning sunshine broke through the trees, awakening Babbity out of a deep sleep.

Today was the day he would look for the relatives of Ruben Willems, the other missing person.

After a hearty breakfast, including porridge, he left the hotel for the Willems' residence which was at the opposite end of Diepenbrockstraat, minutes from the hotel.

All of a sudden he heard an audible voice: *"Prepare! Say the Our Father."*

Babbity did as he was told, remembering that he had the Blessed Oil in his pocket that Father John had given him.

"Say the Armour Prayer," continued the authoritative voice.

Again Babbity did as he was told, but then came the usual quizzical questions: "And what was that all about?"

There was no reply.

He asked again: "What's this all about?"

"When it happens, you will know!" came the reply.

Babbity turned left into Diepenbrockstraat. Ruben's house was only yards away.

It was in another small block of flats near the canal. He spoke into the intercom: "I need to speak to the Willem's family."

The door opened gradually, releasing an overwhelming smell of stale tobacco. Babbity heard internally: "*Spirit of nicotine.*"

A small thin man with dark brooding eyes stared at him with evil intent.

He growled: "What about Ruben?"

Babbity decided to get straight to the matter. He said: "He's dead. The police in Scotland have checked his DNA and I have the unpleasant task of informing the Rubens' family."

The thin man led Babbity through to the main room.

The corridor walls were stained brown in colour from excessive smoking and drug taking.

The thin man said: "He deserves to be dead. Never once did he listen to me."

Babbity asked: "Was he your brother?"

"Yea," came the surly reply.

Babbity thrust the missing person's form into the strangers hand and asked him to sign it.

Reluctantly, he scribbled his name which was a capital L!

Babbity asked out of curiosity: "What does the L stand for?"

"It means Legion, because we are Legion," said the stranger.

Babbity put the form into his pocket. He was about to leave when he felt an overwhelming urge to bless the stranger with his holy oil.

As quick as a flash he brought out his small crucifix and blessed oil and touched the stranger's head with it.

He went berserk! He fell over and started to writhe about on the floor.

"*No, I will never come out of him,*" screamed the demon within.

Wretching and coughing the demon began to spew forth a green horrible bile. The smell was like sulphur.

Babbity felt the Holy Spirit surge through him.

In an order of command, he stretched out his hand with the Crucifix and shouted: "In the name of Jesus Christ come out of him NOW."

Nothing happened.

Babbity poured some Holy Water he was carrying over the writhing figure.

The stranger went crazy again and he tried to grab Babbity's leg but he moved too quickly, shouting: "How dare you touch me. Come out of him now."

After continually invoking the power of the name of Jesus, Babbity began to notice a gradual reduction in the violent reactions of the demon-possessed stranger.

He tried to stand up but Babbity drenched him again with the Holy Water.

This had a powerful effect. The man fell to the floor and lay motionless.

Babbity continued to pray.

Suddenly the stranger looked up at Babbity and he was smiling.

There was a completely different expression on his face. Gone was the taught skin and demonic stare.

Only a relaxed persona was evident.

"How do you feel?" asked Babbity.

"What happened?" asked the stranger.

"Oh, I just think you needed a little prayer," remarked Babbity.

Babbity reached into his pocket again, and taking out the form he asked the stranger to sign his real name this time.

Babbity watched him write "Oscar Willems".

A smiling Oscar looked quizzically at Babbity and asked why he was soaked with water.

"It's Holy Water, anointed by a priest," replied Babbity.

"I would also advise you to try to find an exorcist priest because you may need follow-up work."

He continued: "You seem to have picked up a spirit of nicotine and house disturbance. Sometimes a demon will latch on to your addictions and saturate you with even more misery. You may find your craving for cigarettes and cannabis has now gone."

Babbity laughed: "Now you can start thinking of decorating again!"

He added: "I will inform the police in Scotland that Ruben's family are now aware of what happened to him."

Oscar grabbed Babbity's hand and shook it warmly. "Thank you, thank you," he said.

Babbity interrupted: "Don't thank me, thank Jesus Christ. He delivered you."

As Oscar led Babbity to the front door he said: "I think you're right, this place does need a good coat of paint!"

Laughter filled the air as they said their goodbyes.

As he made his way to a coffee shop, Babbity said: "Another job done. Time to relax."

Sitting comfortably at a window seat he pondered on what had just happened.

His thoughts were interrupted by the internal voice: *"Now you know why I told you to prepare."*

Babbity said: "You bet, you're in charge!"

"Ah good, surrender," came the reply.

Babbity continued: "Over to you now."

The evening sunlight was now streaming in through the coffee shop window, prompting Babbity to think about home again.

"Only one more day then it's Edinburgh and Alice in wonderland!" he mused.

He spent the last day in Holland relaxing and visiting the Archaeology of The Netherlands permanent exhibition in Leiden.

He marvelled at the Roman artefacts and sculptures. He said: "This will give me plenty to talk about when I see Ruth again."

CHAPTER 10

A surprise waiting

As he made his way through Schippol Airport the following day, Babbity stopped to buy Alice some wooden daffodils. "They will never die!" he laughed.

The short flight was uneventful, and soon Babbity was heading home in a taxi.

It was only mid-day so when he arrived and unpacked his case he phoned Father John. Luckily he was available to meet him at 2pm.

When he arrived Babbity told Father John about the Deliverance work he encountered in Holland. He said: "It seems the Blessed Virgin is leading me into this work. She also told me she would lead me to her Son Jesus."

Father John smiled, took a sip of his coffee and said: "The Blessed Virgin always leads us to her Son. It doesn't surprise me you are now being led into this ministry. I always had the feeling it could happen."

Babbity shrugged and asked: "What happens now?"

Without hesitation Father John replied: "The time is now rapidly approaching when you need to try to find a solid foundation for your beliefs. In other words, you need to settle on a faith that is pleasing to you."

"But where do I start looking?" asked a perplexed Babbity.

"I think it's staring you in the face Babbity, but you just can't see it yet." replied Father John. "Pray about what direction you should take. I'm sure you will get an answer soon.

"It's time for my dinner Babbity. Let me know how things go."

Babbity skipped up Leith Road and headed towards the Mad Hatters Cafe.

When she saw him Alice rushed into his arms.

"I missed you," she said.

"I was only away for a week," replied Babbity.

Alice responded: "A week is a long time when you're in love."

Babbity brought out the wooden daffodils from behind his back. "For you," he said.

"Alice snuggled into Babbity again. "Lovely just lovely," she said. "They would look nice at your favourite spot in the cafe."

She placed the flowers in a crystal vase and sat them at the window ledge which looked directly onto Princess Street.

After a good chat Alice asked Babbity to pick up a magazine from the book store just round the corner.

"And while you're away I'll get your usual coffee," she said.

The shopkeeper handed him Alice's magazine, and just as he was about to leave a book title caught his eye.

It read: "Malcolm Muggeridge."

"I've heard of that guy," Babbity said. "I'm sure he was a famous author and journalist."

He picked up the book and flicked through the pages.

He came across a chapter where Muggeridge was telling the world that after years of studying different faiths and religions he became a Catholic after meeting Mother Teresa and staying with monks in a monastery in Scotland.

Muggeridge said he was fascinated by the strict monastic life but also the joy that emanated from these holy people.

He also commented on the selfless work of Mother Teresa, who dedicated her life to helping the poor and homeless.

Babbity stood gob-smacked.

"I don't believe this is happening!" he said. "Father John was right again. He said it wouldn't take long."

When he arrived back at the cafe Alice said: "You look as though you are in a state of shock!"

"I am," he replied.

Babbity told Alice what had happened. She was shocked too but also delighted.

She said: "I never once tried to influence you regarding what faith direction you should take. I felt because I was Catholic it would be better to leave it up to the Holy Spirit to guide you and not try to draw you towards my faith."

Babbity stayed silent for a few moments then said: "I know all faiths are equal in the eyes of God, and I always questioned the need to actually belong to any particular faith.

"But when you see the profound effect the lives of others in their faith can have it leads me to only one conclusion - that I need to belong to a faith."

Alice, with tears in her eyes, said: "That's something beautiful you have just said Babbity. I think God is calling you in a big way."

Babbity held Alice's hand and said: "I always respected you for not trying to influence me about religion, but I have to say the Holy Spirit has used you in my choice!"

"You've made a choice?" asked Alice excitedly.

"Of course I have. It has to be the Catholic Church."

Alice gave Babbity another big hug, and he gave her a long tender kiss before saying: "Thanks to you my dear and the Holy Spirit. When do I start?"

"Start what?" asked a startled Alice.

"Start becoming a Catholic, of course," replied a bemused Babbity.

Alice responded: "Well, the first thing is to tell Father John about your decision. He will put you in touch with the Rite for Christian Initiation for Adults team. They will lead you through a course which will probably take about a year, could be sooner though depending on how quick you learn."

Babbity rubbed his hands in excitement. "Can't wait to get started, "he said.

Alice remarked: "I would suggest you contact Father John sooner rather than later."

At that Babbity picked up his mobile to phone Father John who was delighted to hear what had happened.

He told him this year's RCIA intake started in two weeks' time and he would inform the team of a new candidate.

After he came off the phone Babbity turned to Alice and said: "It's on. I'm in the programme!"

Alice kissed him tenderly and muttered lovingly: "Welcome aboard."

Babbity finished his coffee and explained to Alice that he planned to visit Ruth in the afternoon for a catch-up.

"Ok darling," said Alice. I'll see you tomorrow."

Babbity phoned Ruth, and when he arrived at her flat she greeted him with a big hug.

Babbity bent down and gave her a kiss on her wrinkled forehead.

"Tea Babbity?" asked Ruth.

Babbity responded: Yes, why not. It has been a good day."

"You seem very chirpy Babbity," said Ruth. "By the way did you manage to visit Leiden and the exhibition when you were in Amsterdam?"

Babbity replied: "Yes, I made a point of going. It was very engrossing. Those Romans did get about!

"However, Ruth, today is a very special day for me. I've found my faith, and now I know what direction I'm going in!"

Babbity took Ruth's hand and smiled: "I've decided to enter the Catholic Church. I've felt it coming over me for a while, and I received a very powerful confirmation today."

Babbity explained the story to Ruth who said: "I'm so glad for you. Although I'm Jewish, and your father was Jewish, we must always remember that we worship the same God."

"That's right," replied Babbity "Even more importantly, it's good to note that Jesus my Saviour was also Jewish, and so was his Mother. Infact, I feel that Mary his Mother had a big hand in my decision today."

"Typical Mother!" laughed Ruth.

Babbity said: "Mary took me deeper into her Son Jesus. While I was in Amsterdam I found out that one of Mary's titles is the Lady of All Nations. She is the Mother of all Faiths."

Babbity continued: "Infact, Ruth she is your Mother, although not your maternal mother. She appeared to Ida Peerdeman in Amsterdam and told her she came because of a miracle that happened in 1345."

"What was the miracle?" Inquired Ruth.

Babbity took a deep breath and replied: "A dying man called for a priest to administer the last rights, but after receiving Holy Communion the man vomited.

"The vomit was subsequently poured on to a nearside burning fire, but in the morning the Holy Communion was found to be completely un-damaged and floating above the fire!

"Other miracles then came to be associated with the Holy Eucharist, and so began the great tradition of the Miracle Procession. A few years later a chapel was built on the site of the miracles."

Ruth looked at Babbity and started to cry.

"Are you alright Ruth?" asked a concerned Babbity.

Ruth wiped the tears from her weary frown and spoke in a whisper:

"That was very touching Babbity, and when you also mentioned *Maternal Mother* my heart skipped a beat!

"I have to share something with you," she said. "There is a reason why I asked you to go to Diepenbrockstraat!

Babbity replied: "Yes, I wondered about that."

Ruth took another sip of tea and sighed saying:

"Did your father's friends in Holland enlighten you about anything?"

"Yes," replied Babbity. "The first thing I found out was that Hugo, the owner of the hotel, was actually my father's brother. So it was nice to know I had another uncle!"

Ruth said: "I wanted you to find that out for yourself Babbity. It might have been too confusing for you otherwise."

She continued: "Did Hugo tell you anything else?"

Babbity glanced at the archaeological drawings on the wall and then looking directly at Ruth:

"Yes, he said he had another brother called Vincent who was called the black sheep because nobody knew about his whereabouts. So I have two uncles I didn't know about!"

Ruth began to breath heavily.

"Are you alright?" inquired Babbity"

Ruth looked at Babbity with saddened eyes and blurted out: "I met Vincent many years ago here in Edinburgh. He came looking for your father Aaron, but he never found him."

Ruth let out a big sigh and continued: "I had a relationship with Vincent. I fell in love with him. I fell pregnant and gave birth to a baby boy."

Babbity's jaw dropped as Ruth continued:

"I lived with Vincent and the child for about six years. We never married. One day he just took off with the boy. At the time we were not getting on too well, but I always thought we could work through it."

Ruth started to cry again. She continued: "I never did trace either Vincent or my boy. I always had a feeling they went back to Holland, and I got information from Hugo to corroborate that."

Babbity put his arms around Ruth. "You poor, poor woman," he said.

Gradually Ruth's tears subsided. She asked Babbity: "Did anything happen in Diepenbrockstraat?"

He said: "Well, when I met a man called Joseph he told me a tragic story about a boy he adopted after the parents split up because of drugs."

"He adopted a boy?" explained Ruth.

Babbity said: "Yes, but he threw him out of the house because of his drug taking. He never saw him again.

"As you know Ruth, it was my job to try to locate the boy."

Ruth asked: "What did he look like?"

Babbity said: "He was about thirteen with a slim build and brown eyes. Why are you asking Ruth?"

She replied: "Can you not see it Babbity? What was the boy's name?"

Babbity, scratching his head, replied: "Lucas"

Ruth was shaking as she stood up and made her way to the toilet.

Babbity drank his tea. Is she ok he thought. She didn't look too great.

Suddenly, the penny dropped.

"Surely, it's not what I'm thinking!" he said aloud.

When Ruth came back she asked Babbity: "Did you find Lucas?"

Babbity said: "Yes, not in Holland, but here in Edinburgh."

"In Edinburgh!" Ruth gasped.

Babbity said: "He was found in the area of the Vaults."

A worried Ruth asked: "Where is he now?"

Babbity began to feel nauseous. He knew in his heart what was about to happen.

"We found the remains of Lucas in the Vaults," he said. "He had been dead for some time."

Ruth began to wail. She was inconsolable. "My boy, my boy," she cried out loud.

Ruth's voice stuttered: "His father Vincent, does he know?"

Babbity shook his head in despair. "I don't think so," he replied.

Ruth sat in silence. She was totally destroyed by the information Babbity had revealed.

She looked at the clock, it was 6pm.

"Maybe I should have a rest now Babbity," she said in a weak voice.

She continued: "Check out Krakow in Poland. Hugo told me that Vincent might be there. If you find him let me know."

Babbity gave Ruth a hug and apologised for being the bearer of bad news.

"It's not your fault Babbity," she said. "It was meant to be. God has revealed this information to me. He must be calling me to my son's side. I truly believe I will meet him again."

Ruth looked at Babbity, and, with tears in her eyes, said: "I'm so sorry I will not see your children Babbity. You're a fine young man. Remember to tell Vincent I still love him."

Babbity turned around and walked away, but he had the impulse to look back at Ruth. She smiled lovingly at him and said: "Remember me as loving you."

Then she closed the door.

The following morning Babbity got a call from Constable Baxter.

"I hear you're back again," he said.

"Yes, back again to Auld Reekie," answered Babbity.

Baxter continued in a faltering voice: "Do you know Ruth Goldberg, from Princess Street Gardens?"

"Yes, why?" asked Babbity.

Baxter said: "Well, I'm sorry to tell you…she died last night! Her neighbour phoned the station this morning to tell us Ruth had been found dead by the postman. She hadn't locked the door."

Babbity shrieked: "Oh no, Oh no. I loved that old woman. I must have been the last person to see her alive. Oh no!"

"Babbity, I'm so sorry," said Baxter. "Come over and see me."

In total shock Babbity dropped his phone. As he picked it up, he heard a familiar voice:

"There is power in the name of Jesus. Come to me and I will give you strength. Ruth is with me now. Her suffering ensured this."

Babbity composed himself again before asking: "Constable Baxter are you still there?"

He replied: "Yes Babbity, everything alright?"

"Just dropped my phone, that's all."

"Pop in when you can," replied Baxter.

"I will," said Babbity.

CHAPTER 11

The diary

Babbity was still upset at Ruth's death when he went to see Alice in the cafe.

"Ruth died last night," he cried. "The police phoned me."

Alice held him in her arms. They were both lost in their grief.

Babbity spoke about meeting Ruth in Jerusalem and how he had felt a love for her.

"She's in a better place now Babbity," said Alice.

Babbity shrugged his shoulders, saying: "I'm meeting Father John. I'm sure he can say a prayer with me."

"That's the spirit," replied Alice.

Later that day Babbity explained to Father John all that had happened.

The priest said powerful prayers over him, and explained that his emotional state would start to improve.

Babbity felt so much better after the prayer session.

He said: "I think I will visit Constable Baxter and give him my report."

Father John said: "Good idea Babbity, keep in touch."

Babbity drove to the police station and met Baxter in his office.

"You've had quite a welcome back to Edinburgh," said a sympathetic Baxter.

Babbity shrugged. "Yea, it's par for the course with me," he said.

Baxter changed the subject by asking about the missing person reports.

"How did it go?" he asked.

"It all went well," said Babbity. "The families of the missing persons were located. Case now closed for those two."

He explained the background to each case, but deliberately missed out the Deliverance session. For another time he thought.

Baxter looked through the file and asked: "Any ideas where to next?"

Babbity replied: "Funnily enough, I know already. Krakow in Poland!"

"Let's have a look," said Baxter as he rifled through the file.

He continued: "Ah here we are. There's only one person this time. His name is Piotr Weitch. His family live in Krakow's main square, near a large church called Saint Mary's."

He asked: "Do you know that area?"

Babbity smiled saying: "A few years ago I worked in a place called Wloclawek, which is about three hours' drive from Warsaw. We visited Krakow, so I'm fairly familiar with the city. What are the details of the missing guy?"

Baxter responded: "He was 50 and had been missing for 10 years. He was 6ft 2 inches tall, slim build, black curly hair and green eyes.

Baxter continued: "Here's the file. The sooner you leave the better. The inspectors are starting to push me for closure on all of these cases."

Babbity said: "Will let you know how this goes." He picked up the file and made his way to the car.

A few days later he was eating his breakfast when the telephone rang.

"Is this Babbity Bowster?" asked the caller.

"Yes, and who are you?" replied Babbity.

My name is David Goldberg. I'm a rabbi. Can I visit you today, it's very important.

Babbity answered "Yes, I will be here all day."

"Two o'clock suit?" asked the rabbi.

"Yes, that's fine. See you then," replied Babbity.

A sharp knock at the door announced the arrival of Rabbi David.

Babbity shouted: "Come in, the doors open."

David Goldberg was in his 70s. He was heavy round the waistline and looked unshaven. His glasses looked like the bottom of two glass soda bottles!

"Sit down please," said Babbity. "Coffee?"

"No, I've had enough today," said Rabbi David.

"Well what can I do for you?" asked Babbity.

"I'll cut straight to the chase. I'm the brother of Ruth Goldberg. Did you know she left a will?"

"No," gasped a bewildered Babbity.

"Well she left you something unusual," replied Rabbi David.

"She left you her private diary. She also said you can take any item you wish to have from her flat!"

Babbity was stunned.

"That's certainly unusual, a private diary?" remarked Babbity.

"I can tell you that has caused consternation among the family," said David.

"I'll bet!" replied Babbity.

"We're clearing her flat, so I would appreciate if you could come to the house as soon as possible to pick up the diary."

"No problem. How about tomorrow, is that ok?" asked Babbity.

"Perfect. See you then Mr Bowster," replied Rabbi David as he left.

Babbity slumped on the couch.

"Why is it that I get into these situations?" he mused.

"Because you are open," replied the Holy Spirit audibly.

"Open to what?" asked Babbity.

"To my Spirit!" came the reply.

Babbity made himself another coffee. He then phoned Alice to tell her about Ruth's will. Alice said: "She must have really trusted you Babbity. What an honour. Don't question it. Accept it as a gift from God."

"Ok dear, I'll trust you on that one," replied Babbity.

CHAPTER 12

A shock

The following day Babbity was greeted by Rabbi David as he arrived at Ruth's flat.

Most of the antique furniture had already been removed.

"Ah here it is, Mr Bowster….the diary," said Rabbi David.

It was bound in a deep-tan coloured leather and intricately styled with superb stitching. It looked to be very old and well used.

"It's yours," said David. "She must have really liked you."

"Yes, we were soul mates," replied Babbity as he ran his finger round the outer edges of the locked diary.

"Here's the key Mr Bowster. I've kept it safe for you. You can be sure nobody has opened it. It's for your eyes only."

Rabbi David continued: "Ah yes, she wanted you to pick a gift from these."

He walked into Ruth's bedroom and pointed to a collection of statues.

"Take your pick," he said.

Shock came over Babbity, but then his eyes fell immediately on a statue of the Virgin Mary.

He pointed to the statue. "I'll have that one," he said.

Rabbi David picked the statue up and handed it to Babbity saying: "Is it the mother of Jesus?"

Babbity looked at the statue again, saying "Yes, it looks familiar. In fact, it says below the base…. Akita."

"Ah Japan," replied Rabbi David. "I remember Ruth spoke about her visits to Japan. She said she felt a certain holiness in Akita."

Babbity looked at Rabbi David and was prompted to say: "Jesus allows his mother to appear to the world!"

There was silence.

Then Rabbi David exclaimed: "I know he does."

Further silence.

Continuing, Rabbi David astounded Babbity saying: "I had a Messianic experience many years ago. I know Jesus is Yeshua!"

Babbity nearly dropped the diary!

"That's a powerful thing to say," replied Babbity.

"It's true Jesus *is* the Messiah!" proclaimed Rabbi David.

Babbity looked at him in surprise and said: "I think we will be seeing each other again."

"That would be a good idea," replied Rabbi David.

He carefully packed away the Akita statue and handed it to Babbity. He said: "Take care for now. Watch over the statue. Here are my contact details. Stay in touch."

Babbity accepted the statue graciously and left the near-empty flat soon after.

As soon as he arrived back home he opened the diary.

A note lay inside the first page. It read:

"My Dear Babbity, by now you will have learned of my death.

"From the moment I met you in Jerusalem I felt at ease with you. You have a rare gift of openness. This openness will lead to vulnerability, but it is much better to be open than closed.

"I have travelled to many countries. I have experienced many trials and tribulations, and you know all about Vincent and Lucas.

"I hope these private revelations will inspire you on to great things. Remember that the greatest of all gifts is love. I truly experienced that love with Vincent and Lucas.

"I will pray for you in Heaven. And I will be patient there waiting for Vincent. Tell him these things.

Finally, I always remember reading a great book by St Augustine who said:

"To fall in love with God is the greatest of all romances; to seek him the greatest adventure; and to find him the greatest human achievement.

"Take care, until we meet in Heaven. Your friend Ruth."

Babbity started to cry. "Where are all these tears coming from?" he bubbled.

"Get yourself together. There is too much work to do."

He slept well that night. He didn't open the diary proper; he felt the need to digest Ruth's loving words first.

The following day he booked the flights and hotel for Poland.

He would be leaving in six weeks' time. This would give him plenty of time to get settled in with the RCIA course.

"Poland! I don't believe it. What have you in store for me this time dear Lord," he exclaimed.

VOLUME 5

(Babbity Bowster meets the Scarred Woman)

CHAPTER 1
Opening the diary

Babbity sat in his high-backed office chair, tapping a pencil on his desk in pensive thought.

Alice, who had just come in to visit him, was in listening mode.

"You know when I was in Holland," said Babbity, "I came across some interesting information in Leiden.

"For instance, the Pieterskerk was the church of the Pilgrim Fathers before sailing on the Mayflower to the New World.

"Leiden was also home to the Scots Presbyterian community during the Restoration period."

Alice interrupted: "Interesting!"

Babbity continued: "A commemorative plaque to the Pilgrim Fathers in the Pieterskerk reads:

But now we are all, in all places, strangers and pilgrims travellers and sojourners.

"You know Alice that plaque resonated with me. I instantly realised I was a traveller in Holland, and yet I also felt I was beginning a pilgrimage towards Jesus and his Mother."

Alice leaned over and held Babbity's hand. She said: "The Holy Spirit will always touch your heart, when it is open."

With a cheeky smile he said: "Talking about spirits, how about a mid-day tipple?"

"Sounds like a good idea," replied Alice.

During lunch in a local resturant Babbity explained everything to Alice, especially the shock of being left the personal diary of Ruth Goldberg.

"And what do you think about the statue from Akita? I've already checked it out. It's the exact same as the picture of The Lady of all Nations.

"There is a connection," he added. "In the 1960s a priest said the prayer of The Lady of all Nations over a nun who was seriously ill. She was miraculously cured.

"In recognition of this a sculptor carved the image of *The Lady* in wood.

"The Mother of Jesus began speaking to another nun through the statue! The name of the congregation was the Sisters of the Handmaids of the Eucharist. The statue also bled 101 times. The blood was analysed. It was human blood."

Babbity added: "Amazing."

Alice nodded in agreement.

The couple left the restaurant after cosying up to one another and planning their fuure.

Sitting at his desk the following evening in his flat Babbity slotted the key into the well-made mechanism. The diary sprung open.

It was almost as if Ruth was welcoming him with open arms!

"What about my diary?" uttered an unknown female voice.

"Oh no, here we go again!" said Babbity, but there was no further response.

The first page of the diary was dated May, 1945. The writing said: "I was released from Auschwitz today!"

The next entry read: "For as long as I live I will never disclose anything about my time here in this death camp. Only through this diary will there be any revelations."

Ruth continued in her writings: "Many times I questioned the existence of God as my heart was troubled watching the daily slaughter of innocents.

"How can this be? Where is God?

"And yet a deep intuition within me would take my eyes to a sunset after a hot day. My troubled mind would be instantly comforted knowing that Hashem had made that glorious sun.

"Lord, if I ever leave here take my hand and guide me throughout my life. Take me where you want to take me. My life is in your hands."

Babbity became emotional imagining the horrors of Auschwitz.

"You're coming to Poland aren't you?" said the audible voice.

Babbity replied in a stuttering voice: "Yes"

"Well, you will see Auschwitz for yourself," was the reply.

"Who are you?" asked Babbity.

There was no reply.

"Information, then nothing," said Babbity. "It's almost as if a veil covers the revelations!"

He sat in the silence, contemplating the words of Ruth.

"How must she have felt?" he thought.

CHAPTER 2

A chance encounter

The flight to Krakow took around three hours, and Babbity fell asleep for most of it.

During his sleep he was shown an image of the Virgin Mary, but he couldn't discern what it meant or where it was leading him to.

He was awakened by the stewardess: "Can you put your seat in the upright position," she asked as the plane came in to land.

As he made his way through departures his memory was jolted when he saw the inverted triangle-glass frontage.

"Ah, I remember now," he said.

He took a taxi to the city centre. His hotel was located in the area of Rynek Glowny, which was in the main square of Krakow facing the Basilica of St Mary.

Babbity had fond memories of working in Poland many years before.

He noticed a big change in the main square which had many more restaurants.

He studied the Basilica of St Mary's and thought "really need to visit this church".

During his thought process, a crippled beggar tugged at his trouser leg asking: "Mercy sir, have mercy on me."

Babbity reached into his pocket and gave him a 50 Zloty note.

"Thank you, the Lord will reward you," said the beggar as he crawled away to a local shop to buy some food.

Babbity decided to visit the Jewish quarter. On his way he passed a shop with an interesting picture in the window.

"That's the Lady I saw in my dream on the plane," he said. "The Black Madonna, but I've never heard of it!"

Spotting a nice little eatery he decided to have a bite to eat.

The cafe was called the Hamsa, Hummus and Happiness. "What a nice name," he thought.

On the menu were platters of olives, baby ghanoush, flat breads and hummus. He called the Arabic waiter: "Just my type of food," he said.

"Would you like a mixed platter sir?" asked the waiter.

"Yes, you read my mind!" replied an eager Babbity.

Looking round the décor of the café he was astonished to see a photograph on a wall of his uncle Hugo from Holland!

He stood up and moved closer for a better look. "Yes, its really him!" he said.

Babbity turned around when a gentle hand on his shoulder disturbed his concentration.

The person looking at him was tall and handsome and was in his late eighties.

"You looked puzzled sir," said the elderly waiter.

Babbity stood back, still a bit bewildered.

The waiter enquired: "Can I help you?"

A shocked Babbity sat down at his table and said: "That picture, that's my uncle!"

Now it was the turn of the waiter to sit down.

"It's your uncle?" he queried.

"Yes. it's my uncle Hugo and I recently visited him in Holland."

The waiter paused then said: "You won't believe this but my name is Vincent. I am Hugo's brother!"

A shocked Babbity immediately saw the resemblence to the Davidoff family.

Babbity, with his mouth wide open in surprise, said: "You're his brother!"

"Yes," replied Vincent.

He stared at Babbity intently. His smile changed to a serious frown as he asked: "Why are you here in Poland?"

"I'm on official business," he replied.

"But tell me, how did you end up here in Poland? I was told by Ruth…"

"Ruth!" interrupted Vincent. "How do you know her?"

Babbity said: "I'm going to tell you the whole story, so I think you should take a little break from your duties. This could take some time!"

Vincent said: "That's ok, I own the place. Just take your time."

Babbity explained how he had met Ruth in Jerusalem, "and she told me she had fallen in love with you".

Vincent replied: "I loved her, but it didn't work out.

"We had a son together, but he started to witness our arguing so I felt it would be better if we both left."

Babbity said: "That was the hardest part for Ruth, taking the boy away," said Babbity.

There was silence.

Vincent looked at Babbity with tears in his eyes: "I know, I now realise it was selfish of me."

More silence.

The arabic music seemed to impose on the solemnity of the moment as Babbity asked: "Your son, where did he go?"

Vincent replied: "After a couple of years in Holland he kept pleading to return to Edinburgh.

"I told him it was impossible. That's when he began to mix with the wrong crowd.

"One morning I woke up and he was gone! He took all his belonnings. I never saw him again. I tried to find him but it was useless."

Babbity shook his head for he knew what was coming.

He said: "Your son did make it to Edinburgh; he must have been searching for Ruth."

Babbity then told Vincent he was a special constable in Scotland assigned to the missing persons' branch.

He added: "One of those missing persons, with the name of Piotr Weitch, lives here in Krakow. I have to find the family to let them know their son is dead!"

Vincent then said: "So you're saying you knew my son went to Edinburgh."

"That's right," replied Babbity.

He said: "I found human bones in a place called the Vaults in Edinburgh by a process of elimination and DNA techniques.

"I'm sorry to tell you Vincent that some of those bones were your sons. He was called Lucas Janssen."

Vincent cried out: "My son dead!"

Babbity took his hand.

"I'm afraid so," he said.

A distraught Vincent was in tears. "Why did I let him go. Why?"

After a few minutes of reflection, Babbity asked Vincent: "Why did you change your second name?"

Vincent blurted out: "I thought I would start a new life with Lucas, so I needed a new identity."

Babbity nodded. "That was puzzling me because I know our family name is Davidoff."

After a pause Vincent asked: "So you're a Davidoff too? But why did you come to the Jewish quarter? Our meeting was a million to one chance!"

Babbity, shaking his head, replied: "I know, I know, it was just a hunch. I already knew you were in Krakow and I thought the best place to look was in the Jewish quarter."

He added: "Maybe it's spiritual too. I sometimes feel a presence guiding me."

Vincent smiled and said: "Yes, I still have my beliefs too. I visit the synagogue regularly."

Babbity then took a large gulp of coffee before informing Vincent that Ruth had only recently passed away.

Vincent was silent. He whispered: "Sometimes we try to run away from life, but we can never run away from the memories. May Hashem have mercy on me! That's Lucas and now Ruth. I will forever have this on my mind."

There was nothing Babbity could say. The grief on Vincent's face said it all!

After another long silence Vincent asked: "My brother Hugo is he well?"

"Yes," replied Babbity, "I'm sure he would welcome you if you got in touch."

"It has been a long time," replied Vincent, "but I think I will do just that."

He added: "You know Babbity, I came through a really bad patch in my life when Lucas left. He was only ten years of age.

"I realised I had to change. This restaurant was a gift from God. I know that now. And look what happens, I meet you here. It has to be in God's plan.

"Please come back to see me Babbity. You will always be welcome."

Before parting, Vincent had one final question: "Who looked after Lucas in Holland?"

Babbity replied: "A man called Joseph Starsky found your son homeless in the Diepenbrockstraat area of Amsterdam and eventually adopted him, but Lucas left, never to return."

Vincent wept again, prompting Babbity to hold him in his arms. It was a solemn moment for both of them.

As Babbity wandered into the sultry warm air of Kazimierz he was amazed at what had just happened.

"What a coincidence," he thought. "No, not a coincidence, this is a God incidence. Nothing is impossible for God, nothing!"

CHAPTER 3

A luminous green arc

Babbity passed the shop with the Black Maddona picture in the window.

He stopped and stared at the captivating image.

"Come to me," uttered an audible female voice.

"Who is this?" Babbity asked.

As in previous experiences, there was no immediate reply.

Next to the image was a photograph of a beautiful large steepled church in a place called Jasna Gora.

Babbity was so captivated with it he said: "I need to go there."

The shop was next to a piece of vacant ground where Babbity noticed an elderly lady sitting on a rock staring at him.

She was dressed in black tattered clothing and looked to be analysing his movements.

She leered at Babbity shouting: "Stay away from her!"

Dragging a stick of wood through the red dusty soil, and with an angry expression she repeated: "I said stay away from her!"

"Who are you?" asked Babbity in a commanding voice.

The old woman laughed at him and said: "I am from the dark skies. My life is guided by the charcoal hands of my followers."

Babbity thought back to what Aaron had told him in Jerusalem: "You have the authority of Jesus. Always remember to use his name when dealing with dark forces."

He sprung in to action.

He removed a small bottle of Holy Water from his tweed jacket and splashed it over the old woman.

"In the Name of Jesus of Nazareth, Son of the Living God, I command you to come out of her," he said.

The old woman started to writhe on the soil, spitting a horrible yellow liquid from her mouth.

Her screams sounded like a wolf crying at night.

Babbity continued to pour Holy Water over her, shouting: "Out, out, Fire of the Holy Spirit envelop her."

He noticed the woman's hands had returned to normal, but he continued: "Fire, Fire, Fire of the Holy Spirit. Fire."

Similar to other exorcisms Babbity had witnessed, she started to wriggle about like a snake, her eyes blood red.

"No, I won't come out of her she's mine," came the reply.

"I am from Hell. My name is Beelzebub. She's mine, and I won't leave her.

Babbity responded: "Remember, Jesus is here. He is looking at you. He wants you to come back to Him."

Amid further screams he poured over more Holy Water, and breathed out forcefully into her face proclaiming confidently: "Receive the Holy Spirit. Jesus is now in charge of your life."

She suddenly stood up, smiling. Her haggard face turned into a serene expression and her blue eyes were bright and full of life.

She looked at Babbity and her wrist watch asking: "Where have I been for the last thirty minutes?"

He grabbed her hand and said: "Welcome back to Jesus, you have been in a dark place."

The old woman fell into Babbity's arms and began to weep tears of joy. She sighed: "I feel as if someone has lifted a heavy and dark burden from me."

Babbity replied sympathetically: "Yes, Jesus has taken your inner demons away. Now he wants you to follow Him instead of the occult."

A sound of hands clapping enveloped Babbity and the old woman.

Babbity turned to see a group of young men in priestly vestments applauding his efforts.

"We were praying for you when we saw what was happening," said one of them.

He continued: "We are student priests from Jasna Gora!"

Babbity shook hands with them muttering: "That name again!"

The delivered woman could only smile in thankfulness at what had just happened.

After conversing with the seminarians Babbity said: "See you in Jasna Gora."

He and the old woman headed off to a coffee shop. He inquired of her name.

"Maria," she replied.

"Very apt!" said Babbity. "Do you know Maria is the mother of Jesus?"

"Yes, I know that," she said.

Maria looked at Babbity and began to cry. She said: "I had a great devotion to Mary as a child, but in my fifties I met a group of occult people who swayed my head with a lot of powerful arguments about walking away from Jesus and Mary. Unfortunately, I believed them."

Babbity said: "All I can say is that today you met the right people. First of all Jesus and his Mother and secondly myself."

Babbity looked at Maria and added: "There are similarities between your story and mine.

"My mother was an atheist and my father a Jew. I never took an interest in religion. My mother always came out with the great lie 'if there was a God then why does he allow wars and poverty.'

"My escapade with the occult came when I was on a tourist trail in my home town of Edinburgh.

"I was at the end of the group looking at the underground vaults in a series of tunnels below the South Bridge in central Edinburgh.

"I can remember being surrounded by three ugly looking ogres. 'Come with us' they said. 'Satan has a plan for you.'"

Taking a deep breath Babbity continued: "I foolishly followed them.

"Further down the tunnel complex I was introduced to their leader, a truly horrible beast called Gash. At first he was so pleasant and persausive. He asked me to join them and I did.

"Within about half an hour I had said a consecration prayer to Satan - and that was me trapped."

Maria interrupted: "That's exactly what happened to me. I was involved in a secret blood ritual, offering myself to Beelzebub."

Babbity continued: "Once that consecration is done, the evil one takes over. Those demons within that tunnel complex were manifesting themselves at Satan's command. Just the same way that Satan can make his followers de-materialise too.

"They gave me certain tasks to accomplish, calling them the curse of the 500 pennies, which meant I had 500 missions to complete before I could be released from my curse."

Babbity continued: "I had completed many of those awful tasks, such as being involved with marriage break-ups and divorce.

"Then my sister Mhairi died suddenly. I was devastated because she had been a great source of solace to me throughout my life.

"I had a violent character, being involved in many street fights. Basically I was just a bully. I didn't know any other way of life.

"I had to get away from Edinburgh and Scotland because of my sister's death, so I went to the Seychelles in the Indian Ocean.

"I visited the beautiful island of Praslin. However, my nightmares continued.

"Whilst I was there I found five dead bodies on the beach. They were all female, aged about thirty.

"It later transpired they had been lured into an all-woman occult group, and their deaths were the result of a powerful spell put on to them by the leader of the group."

Maria interupted again: "Yes, my leader was powerful too."

Babbity looked at her peacefully: "But Jesus is more powerful, always remember that.

"When I returned from the Seychelles my leader Gash was none too pleased about my disappearance, but I managed to get away with it.

"To cut a long story short, I met an exorcist priest who prayed over me with his group.

"The exorcism lasted over two hours, and through the power of Jesus I was finally delivered from the demons that had infected me in the vaults.

"So now you see why we have been brought together Maria. Jesus wanted me to tell you my story, to bring you hope.

"This is no coincidence, it's a God incidence. I thank God Almighty that through my deliverance prayers you have finally been freed.

"Sometimes deliverance prayers and exorcisms can go on for years, but in your case it lasted just over thirty minutes. God has stepped in quickly Maria; he wants you to be freed today for a reason."

"What's the reason?" asked a baffled Maria.

"I think Jesus is going to use you in a powerful way. Maybe you will help to pray against the occult, or even be involved in deliverance yourself.

"Anyway, that will all be revealed to you in due course. What you have to do now is visit the sacraments frequently, especially Holy Mass and Confession. That way your soul will be sustained with the grace of the Holy Spirit."

Babbity took a deep breath and asked: "When I was praying over you I saw a dark sky with a feint luminous green arc and horrible face. Does that mean anything to you?"

"Yes," replied Maria. "The occult group I was attached to worshipped the dark sky and the creatures of the green luminous night.

"Sometimes those creatures would materialise from dark powder."

Babbity said: "Ah, that's why I saw the guy with the crumbling dark ash arms."

Maria replied: "That's correct Babbity. It was probably horrible to witness, but to us it was just normal!"

Babbity asked: "Where do you live Maria?" Babbity asked:

"Jasna Gora," she replied.

"Not that name again," said Babbity.

Maria continued: "We hated that church and all it stood for. Those miraculous healings put a cloud over our group. But now I know why. I will now try to dedicate my life to Jesus, through the help of his mother."

Babbity said: "It has been a privilege for me to witness and be involved in your deliverance. I will pray for you always.

"Hopefully we can meet when I come to Jasna Gora. However, remember your occult leader will probably sense something good has happened to you, so stay away. Join a prayer group and they will be able to give you ongoing support and advice."

Maria took Babbity's hand tenderly and kissed his cheek saying: "Thank you so much. I will keep you informed about the next stage of my development.

"I will always remember this day. See you in Jasna Gora."

Maria walked away confidently turned round, smiled and waved at Babbity. Then she was gone.

Babbity was now with his thoughts: "My Lord and My God, thank you for your help today. Please guide Maria in her new life."

CHAPTER 4

The meeting

That very night after meeting Maria, Babbity had a vivid and varied dream sequence.

He could see a small section of wall about 12 feet high, with about 12 rounded semi circle tops. Each vertical slot was about half a metre wide with grey coloured plaster on the outside. There was a display sign, but he wasn't able to read the contents, although 1941 to 1943 was visible.

The dream then changed to the fluttering pages of a diary!

He could see written on the pages wording that seemed to describe profound spiritual experiences and details of apparitions.

The dream sequence ended with a horrific scene.

Babbity was aware of standing in a room next to people who were using human skin as lamp shades.

At this point he woke up sweating.

"What was that all about?" he said.

A female voice whispered in reply: *"This will unfold!"*

Babbity looked around the room but could see nobody.

When he was fully awake he decided to search for the family of Piotr Weitch, whose last known address was in the famous Krakow square, adjacent to St Mary's Basilica.

The block of flats looked stylish with red tiling on the roofs and white painted walls and windows. The building was on five different levels.

Babbity pressed the buzzer for the Weitch family.

"Gindobre," came the reply from the intercom.

Babbity answered: "Hello, I'm from Scotland. Is this the home of the Weitch family?"

"Go away," was the rude answer.

Babbity persevered: "I need to speak to you. I have information about Piotr."

He's no son of mine," shouted a woman.

A few moments of silence passed when suddenly the front door to the apartment swung open and Babbity made his way to the Weitch household on the fourth floor.

A woman in her late 80s stood there with socks rolled down to her ankles. She had no teeth and looked like the wicked witch from Snow White!

She glared at Babbity.

"What have you to tell me?" she grumbled.

"Do you know Piotr," asked Babbity sympathetically.

She paused for a few seconds then replied: "He is my son."

She added: "I haven't seen him for over 10 years. He left the family when he was about 40 years old, trying to seek his fortune elsewhere. He never kept in contact."

Babbity took the missing persons' report from his briefcase and showed it to the elderly lady.

He said: "We have found bones that match the DNA of the Weitch family. The police here in Poland have confirmed that. I'm sorry to tell you that Piotr is dead."

"I will let the family know," she said.

Babbity asked her to sign the release form. Her name was Gosia Weitch.

Babbity said: "Thanks Gosia for your help in this awful matter. I will inform the Polish and Scottish police that this case is now closed. We will send Piotr's ashes if needed."

"Don't bother," she replied and slammed the door!

Back at the hotel Babbity planned his strategy for the rest of his visit.

He wondered about the previous night's dream.

"Three separate sections to the dream. Does that mean three separate places?" he asked. "Where do I go first to unravel these revelations?"

The following day Babbity got a quick reply to his question.

As he strolled around the streets next to Krakow main square he noticed small tourist go-carts which had different destinations written on the side. The first he saw had "Krakow Ghetto Wall." Next to that was "Schindler's Factory!"

"Wow! Schindler's Factory, from the graveyard in Jerusalem to this. What a journey," he said.

"Don't forget Lagiewiniki," came an audible female voice.

Once again Babbity looked around, but there was nobody there!

The voice continued: *"The diary."*

That was part of his dream. "Lagiewniki has to be a clue," he said.

As Babbity studied the tourist cabs, he suddenly received a vision of Aaron, his father. He was smiling at him.

Then Babbity spoke: "The lampshades, made from human skin. Auschwitz!"

Suddenly it dawned on Babbity.

"That's it," he said. The three places - the Krakow Ghetto Wall, Lagiewniki and Auschwitz!

"Thank you dear Lord for revealing these things to mere children. I'm glad to be a child of God.

CHAPTER 5
It's only five minutes away

Babbity asked one of the cab drivers how far it was to the Krakow Ghetto Wall, his first choice.

"Only five minutes from here. Jump in," he replied.

Many were standing in prayer when Babbity arrived.

Babbity studied the ghetto wall. It was indeed built to resemble gravestones, and it was a sign to the detainees that death was their only escape.

Babbity prayed for the many thousands of Jews who died within the walls from either malnutrition or murder by the Nazis.

As he departed he felt a cold shrill flow through him.

Babbity's next port of call was Lagiewniki, only a twenty minute tram ride from the wall.

When he entered the pilgrimage centre the first thing he noticed was a large picture of a nun. Her name was St Faustina.

Below her face was a photograph of a diary.

"My diary," said a tender female voice.

Babbity walked over for a closer look. The nun was quite young and she had a contented but powerful expression of love.

"Its got to be the diary I saw in the dream," he said.

After he studied the picture he noticed a sign that read: "To the sanctuary."

As he entered it a picture caught his eye of Jesus striding forward with rays of red and white light streaming from his heart.

At the bottom of the picture were the words "Jesu Ufam Tobie - Jesus I Trust in You."

Babbity fell to his knees, and a familiar voice said: *"It was my diary. I am St Faustina, the Apostle of Mercy. Read my diary!"*

Almost immediately, Jesus spoke to him too: *"I am the Divine Mercy. I came to you in Jerusalem. Now I am revealing myself to you, through my secretary, here in her shrine. Do what is required."*

Babbity was stunned. First St Faustina had spoken to him and now Jesus.

He sat in silence for a long while before leaving.

He purchased "The diary" of St Faustina at a shop, and then made his way back to the hotel.

CHAPTER 6
Schindler's factory

After breakfast the following day Babbity took the short ride by buggy to Oscar Schindler's factory.

Ever since his visit to Schindler's graveside in Jerusalem he always knew this would happen.

No matter what Oscar Schindler's lifestyle had been, Babbity was convinced God utilised this man's amazing courage and intellect to free so many Jewish people from bondage.

During the three hours Babbity spent at the factory he watched cinema footage of the Jewish ghetto people being rounded up for deportation to death camps.

That horrible day in 1939 when the German war machine marched into Poland was also recorded with actual radio transmissions of the invasion.

Throughout his visit Babbity came to know Schindler in a deeper way.

He was raised in a Catholic family. His father was a German industrialist and a member of the Nazi party. One of the main reasons he joined the Nazis was because he knew it made good business sense.

Schindler, who died on October 9, 1974, at the age of 66 after a life of failed businesses and marriages, saved 1,200 Jews from extermination.

He was well respected by the Jewish nation, culminating in Stephen Spielberg's film "Schindler's List" telling of his remarkable life.

Babbity wished he could have met him in real life.

CHAPTER 7

Czestochowa

Babbity's trip to Poland was coming to an end, but before it did he had a burning desire to visit the shrine of Jasna Gora in Krakow.

He was drawn to the mysterious Black Madonna. The scar on her face seemed to bring a magnetic feeling of emotional attachment.

It's almost as if he felt she needed his help because of this disturbing mark.

During the two-hour bus journey to Czestochowa, Babbity started to read the Diary of St Faustina.

He was amazed at the promises contained within the book.

One of the most powerful came directly from Jesus.

If a person said a special nine-day novena to the Divine Mercy of Jesus, starting on Good Friday and culminating on Divine Mercy Sunday with Mass, Confession and Holy Communion, every sin committed was completely forgiven.

Babbity was astonished.

As he continued reading he realised he certainly made the right decision to become a Catholic.

St Faustina was only a teenager when Jesus appeared to her during a social evening of dancing.

Jesus looked at her and asked: "How long must I wait on you?"

So the whole Divine Mercy movement started on a dance floor!

Babbity realised that at any time, in any situation, the Holy Spirit will take charge and break through our stubborn natures.

This one promise from Jesus to forgive every sin was a demonstration to him of the most amazing compassion of the Saviour.

Jesus told Saint Faustina: "Even though your sins be as scarlet my unfathomable Mercy is greater."

St Faustina was only 33 years old when she died, the same age as Jesus when he died.

To this very day millions of Catholics visit the special shrine in Lagiewniki to atone for their sins and marvel at the wonderful promises of Jesus.

As the bus journey continued Babbity looked back over his life and decided he would become a devotee of the Divine Mercy.

"What a promise, every sin I've ever committed is wiped clean! This is certainly for me," he said.

The bus shuddered to a stop bringing Babbity's engaging thoughts to an abrupt end. He was in Jasna Gora.

He had booked a small bed and breakfast near the shrine which would give him ample time to explore the area.

After buying a book on the history of the Black Madonna, he was surprised at the various industrial outlets in Czestochowa. Not only were there iron and steel plants but many other industries including textiles, chemical processing and glass and paper paper manufacturing.

The history of the Black Madonna was no less fascinating.

Tradition holds it that St Luke the Evangelist "wrote" the icon on a cypress table in the home of the Holy Family, and St Helena is said to have located it during her visit to the Holy Land and to have brought it to Constantinople in the fourth century.

The icon was eventually owned by Charlemagne who presented it as a dowry to Prince Lev of Galicia (present day western Ukraine) where it was kept for almost six centuries in the royal palace at Belz.

In 1382 after invading tartars attacked the fortress at Belz, the icon was taken to Czestochowa for safekeeping and where it has remained ever since.

It was damaged by Hussite raiders in 1430 who slashed and attempted to burn the painting, changing the whole visage of what is now referred to as the Black Madonna.

In a sense she is the symbol of Poland herself, scarred but persevering in faith.

At least two attempts were made to repair and restore the scar on the Virgin's face, but through time the scar returned. This was taken as a sign the Madonna wanted the symbol to remain.

Although Babbity couldn't yet receive Holy Communion he made an effort to check Mass times as he had a strong desire to attend.

When he entered the main church door he was amazed at the myriad of side altars.

He joined a crowd rushing to take their places in a small chapel within some wrought iron steel fencing.

It was midday and there was a sense of anticipation.

Babbity squeezed his way to the front of the altar, above which was a large silver plaque.

At the stroke of 12 there was a trumpet fanfare and the plaque started to rise gradually, revealing the Black Madonna in a beautiful pink diamond encrusted head and shoulder veil.

It was so overwhelming Babbity felt a wave of ecstasy sweep through him. He fell on his knees and started to cry.

"Thank you for coming my dear son," whispered the Madonna.

All around him people were crying and shouting in excitement. It was truly a site to behold as a number of priests came out to begin Mass.

When Mass ended Babbity stood in a long procession of people who were meandering their way around the back of the altar to get a closer look at the world-famous icon.

He was almost sure that he seen Maria in the procession.

The eyes of the Black Madonna seemed to follow Babbity as he walked past in respectful silence.

As he emerged at the other side of the altar, he heard the virgin say: "Remember Akita; it is linked to my title in Amsterdam. Go there!"

"Akita, when?" he queried.

"Now!" came the reply from the Madonna.

"Now?" asked Babbity with trepidation.

"Yes now," she replied.

Babbity went into a travel agent when he got back to his hotel and booked a return flight for the following day to Tokyo and then on to Akita.

CHAPTER 8

Land of the Midnight Sun

The flight from Krakow to Tokyo took 28 hours, which gave Babbity ample time to reflect on the sudden change in his plans. It also afforded time for study about Akita.

As the aircraft took off he started to read "The Diary of St Faustina." He was amazed to discover she was not happy about the painted version of Jesus in his Divine Mercy, claiming it did not capture the power and magnificence of his compassionate and tender nature.

She spoke of many trials she had when relating the visions to her mother superior and Father Sopocko, her spiritual director.

It was only when St John Paul 2nd was elected that the process of the acceptance of The Divine Mercy was initiated ; after it was previously banned.

Babbity thought about the history of the Church and how there had been so much tumult over the centuries.

Discerning his decision to join the Catholic Church he wondered what his Protestant friends would think.

He prayed for a few moments, asking for guidance.

The Holy Spirit revealed to him the Church was ONE before the Reformation. Everyone was Catholic (universal).

The major schism began through the endeavours of Martin Luther who took exception to the corruption of men within the Church at that time.

Not the corruption of God, but the corruption of men.

Throughout the centuries corruption in the Church has always been a problem, even to this very day.

After a pause in his thoughts; Babbity began to browse through the book about the supernatural events in Akita.

He soon realised that the link up with Amsterdam and The Lady of all Nations was undeniable.

This was further cemented with the previously known fact that a nun in that special convent in Akita was completely healed from a serious illness when The Lady of all Nations prayer was recited over her.

It suddenly dawned on Babbity, "that's where I have to go".

The convent of the sisters of the Handmaids of the Eucharist was located in (Seitai Hoshikai) Akita Yuzawadai in the north island.

Babbity started to get engrossed in the extraordinary events in Akita.

The apparitions began on June 12, 1973, when Sister Agnes Sasagawa saw a brilliant and mysterious light emanate from the chapel tabernacle.

The same thing happened on each of the two following days.

On June 28 a cross shaped wound appeared on the inside left hand of Sister Agnes, bleeding profusely and causing much pain.

On July 6 she heard a voice coming from the statue of the Blessed Virgin Mary in the chapel where she was praying.

On the same day a few of the sisters noticed drops of blood flowing from the statue's right hand. This happened on four occasions. The blood was analysed at Tokyo University and was found to be of human origin.

The wound on the statue's hand remained until September 29 when it suddenly disappeared, to be replaced by "sweat", especially in the forehead and neck.

Two years later on January, 1975, the statue began to weep and continued to do so at intervals for the next 6 years and 8 months. In total it wept 101 times.

In America the 101 Foundation is named after this powerful phenomenon.

The statue, 3ft in height, was carved from a single block of wood from a Katsura tree. It was made by a sculptor in recognition of the miraculous healing of a nun and it was an exact replica of The Lady of all Nations picture, complete with the Virgin of Amsterdam standing on a globe of the world.

Babbity traced his thoughts back to the small chapel in Amsterdam and his private moments with The Lady of all Nations.

He continued reading this fascinating story.

Sister Agnes received three major messages from the Virgin of Akita containing warnings, such as:

"If men do not repent and better themselves, the Father will inflict a terrible punishment on humanity, the work of the devil will infiltrate even in the church….."

This was a confirmation to Babbity regarding the Schism that he had previously pondered.

On February 27, 1978, Pope Paul V1 approved the "promceeding in judging alleged apparitions and revelations" in Akita.

On April 22, 1984, after eight years of investigations, the Rev John Shojiro Ito, Bishop of Niigata, recognised the supernatural character of the events associated with Akita.

"Wow!" exclaimed Babbity as he closed the book.

As Sister Agnes was still alive at the age of 87 Babbity felt a sense of excitement to know he would be visiting her community, although he didn't know if she was still in residence.

The flight was about half way through so Babbity took a nap. He was awakened later by the stewardess, "Coffee sir."

Afterwards his thoughts were drawn back to the Akita events, in particular the information that was provided about the blood results from the statue.

He noticed the tests had been performed by a Professor Eiji Okuhara who was a physician at the University of Akita. He was part of the Bio Chemistry department.

The professor's results stated the blood sweat and tears were:
Blood….Type B
Sweat….Type AB
Tears…..Type AB

The profession of Bio Chemistry rang a bell of interest with Babbity, but he thought no more of it as the plane landed in Tokyo.

His next journey would be the one-hour flight to Akita, where he had booked into the Apa Hotel Akita Senshukeon, which was a forty minute taxi ride to the Shrine of Our Lady.

When he arrived at the hotel he hit the hay in preparation for an early morning start.

As he awoke the sun was shining, bringing a peace within his soul.

He was soon on his way to the Handmaids of the Eucharist Shrine. When he arrived he entered the gift shop where the on-duty nun spoke English.

"Can I speak to Sister Agnes Sasagawa?" asked an excited Babbity.

The nun replied with a sympathetic smile: "Unfortunately, she is quite elderly and is in seclusion because of her health."

The nun could see the disappointment on Babbity's face and said: "However, I can take you to the chapel where the statue is and you can spend some time there!"

He began to smile again. "That would be lovely sister," he replied.

Babbity was the only person there. He fell on his knees staring lovingly at the statue. He thanked the Blessed Virgin for bringing him to Japan.

Strolling around the gardens afterwards he could sense the awesome connection of the messages of Akita and Fatima in Portugal.

The world could never say The Mother of all Nations wasn't warning everyone about their behaviour, and how to change through reparation and reconciliation.

Babbity spent the afternoon at the shrine and then hailed a taxi back to his hotel.

The following morning he decided to go to Akita University to check out the original blood samples from the statue, but he would need the help of the Blessed Virgin to get access to these historical documents.

On arrival he decided to approach a girl he saw in one of the laboratories to inquire about the original blood sample reports.

He was surprised to see she was not Japanese, and even more surprised to see she resembled Alice, his girlfriend!

"Hello," he said.

The girl, in her mid twenties, jumped back with fright at the intrusion.

"Oh sorry," said Babbity, "I didn't mean to startle you. I was wondering if you could help me. I'm looking for the person in charge of the blood sample records."

"Why do you ask?" she asked.

Babbity immediately recognised the Scottish accent.

He responded: "It's for research I'm doing about Our Lady of Akita, and I know the original samples were sent here for analysis."

Babbity continued: "I just wanted to see the records with my own eyes to help me in my faith journey and to satisfy my curiosity."

"I see," replied the girl.

She continued: "Well, it just so happens this is the blood records department. Can you wait a minute while I speak to my superior."

"Of course," replied Babbity. "That would be great."

Babbity took a seat and prayed fervently to the Virgin of Akita.

The girl arrived back ten minutes later, smiling.

"Your in luck," she said. "I can take you to the blood bank. Anyway, I took pity on you when I realised you were Scottish too!"

As they strolled along the brightly painted corridor towards the blood record department, Babbity asked: "Where in Scotland are you from?"

"Edinburgh," she said.

"I should have known that from your accent," replied Babbity. I'm from Edinburgh too. Sorry I didn't introduce myself earlier. My name is Babbity Bowser.

"That's a strange name!" replied the girl.

"Yes, I was named after a Scottish dance," said Babbity. "I live in Princess Street."

The girl responded: "My name is Sheila Buckley and I live near Rose Street."

When they reached the records office the girl looked out the report by Professor Eiji Okuhara.

Blood….B
Sweat…..AB
Tears…..AB

The samples were still contained in sealed test tubes.

"Amazing, absolutely amazing to see this," said Babbity. "Thank you so much for your help Sheila."

Walking back to the laboratory, Babbity casually said: "Coincidently, you have the same surname as my girlfriend Alice!

Sheila stopped in her tracks and uttered in amazement: "Alice is my sister!"

"What!" exclaimed Babbity. He continued: "I thought there was a strong resemblance. I don't believe it, I just don't believe it. This is incredible. You know Sheila I had a feeling this trip was going to be a surprise package!"

Sheila smiled and said: "I have to get back to my desk, why don't we meet up for a coffee when I finish."

"Great idea," replied a delighted Babbity.

CHAPTER 9
The truth unfolds

When they sat at a local Sushi cafe Babbity looked at Sheila with a puzzled expression and asked:

"Why and how did you end up in Japan?"

With a worried frown Sheila replied: "About four years ago I decided on a gap year from my studies as a bio chemist."

Babbity interrupted: "Ah, I remember now! Alice did mention one of her family was studying bio chemistry."

Sheila continued: "I always had a yearning to come to Japan. I also knew about Akita University. It sounded like a really exciting way to see the world and also enhance my career."

Taking a deep breath Sheila continued: "However, my parents we're dead against it. An argument developed into a really horrible exchange of words, which resulted in me walking out the door."

"So you haven't seen them since?" enquired Babbity.

Sheila burst into tears. She said: "To my shame I never let them know I was in Japan. Time then just seemed to fly by."

Babbity comforted her and asked: "So how did you end up here?"

Sheila replied: "When I applied for the scholarship it was supposed to last a year, but because I excelled at my studies the university offered me a secure position in the bio chemistry department."

Two more coffees arrived. Breaking the mood Babbity asked:

"Have you ever visited the Akita shrine?"

"I'm an atheist," she said. "It's not my scene! You don't believe all that mumbo jumbo, do you?"

Babbity said: "As it happens, I do."

He continued: "When I look at you Sheila I am reminded of myself a couple of years ago. Then I found God after a series of inexplicable events that totally changed me."

Babbity explained his conversion experience with Sheila and how he met her sister.

He took a deep breath and continued : "As tomorrow is my last day in Akita how would you like to come to the shrine with me, just for curiosity purposes only?

Sheila laughed and said: "I always believe in chance. We met, that was chance. You tell me my sister Alice is your girlfriend, that's chance. And it just so happens that I am off work tomorrow, so that's chance. Yea, why not. I'll take another chance and go with you to this shrine, only for a short visit though."

After they parted Babbity said to himself: "This has got to be the Holy Spirit at work!"

CHAPTER 10

Tears

The sun shone the following day as Babbity and Sheila walked through the grounds of the shrine and headed for the chapel.

Babbity headed straight for the statue while Sheila stayed at the back of the chapel, watching intently.

Suddenly Babbity fell to his knees and began to cry. He thought about this self same Blessed Virgin's statue that had wept 101 times and he felt his tears were merging with it.

Gradually his tears subsided, but he could hear weeping behind him.

He was astonished to see Sheila completely engulfed in a powerful emotional release of continual tears.

Babbity gave her a hug, and speaking through the tears she spluttered: "I've got to phone home."

Babbity whispered: "I think the Blessed Mother has touched your heart."

They were both in a daze as they walked away from the shrine.

Sheila broke the perfect silence. She asked Babbity if she could use his phone to call Alice.

Babbity nearly dropped it in the excitement as he dialled her number and passed the phone to Sheila.

"Is that you Alice?"

Alice couldn't believe it!

"Sheila, it's fantastic to hear from you."

But before she could continue with her many questions Sheila interrupted: "Yes, Alice, and you won't believe who is with me!"

A puzzled but excited Alice asked: "Who?"

"Your Babbity!"

Now it was Alice's turn to nearly drop the phone.

"What! How on earth did that happen?"

Sheila quickly handed the phone to Babbity. "You're better at telling her," she said.

Babbity spent the next few minutes telling Alice all that had happened.

He added: "I'll explain it better when I get home in a few days' time. See you then my love."

In her excitement Sheila grabbed the phone and shouted in delight: "Tell Mum and Dad I will be home soon."

Alice was in tears and couldn't wait to break the good news to her parents.

Sheila and Babbity then said their farewells with loving smiles and big hugs.

"See you in Auld Reekie," remarked Babbity.

On the plane back to Krakow Babbity reflected on the amazing journey the Lord had taken him - the way he was drawn into the occult, how his sister's death had led him to the Seychelles and the horrible deaths of five young woman.

And he realised the trips to Jerusalem, Holland, Poland and Japan were a carefully planned sequence of events by the wonderful power of the Holy Spirit, which led him through the deliverance experience in Krakow to the discovery of Alice's sister.

It could only have happened through the guidance and protection of Jesus.

Babbity had one final errand to complete before returning to Edinburgh - a visit to Auschwitz.

The following day he travelled the 45-mile journey by train from Krakow to the death camp.

CHAPTER 11
Work to gain your freedom

Going through his mind as he stepped off the train was what Uncle Hugo had told him about Auschwitz and what his father must have experienced.

Looking at the sign above the entrance gate he felt a gut-wrenching sensation as he read the world-famous words "Arbeit Macht Frei" (Work Makes you Free).

And there was a sense of horror as the guide pointed out various areas of ghoulish interest.

She said: "This is where an orchestra played while the killing went on. The members of the band were inmates of the camp!"

She then pointed to a goal post made of dark wood. "This is where they hung inmates," she said.

On and on it went, horror story after horror story.

Next was the gas chambers and ovens!

Babbity stood in the middle of the concrete gas chamber as the guide pointed to a small opening in the ceiling.

"This is where the Zyklon B gas was inserted," she said.

Babbity finished the tour listening to the statistics: "The SS killed at least 960,000 Jews deported to the camp. The soviet troops found grisly evidence of the horror. About 7,000 starving prisoners were found alive in the camp. Millions of items of clothing were discovered along with 6,350 kg of human hair. The Auschwitz Museum holds more than 100,000 pairs of shoes, 12,000 kitchen utensils, 3,000 suitcases and 350 striped camp garments."

The afternoon was drawing to a close, and on the way back to Krakow Airport to catch the evening flight to Edinburgh he thought about his friend Ruth and the horrors she must have experienced in Auschwitz.

This part of Babbity's experiences was coming to an end and a new one was beginning as he made his way from Edinburgh airport to the Mad Hatters Cafe and the love if his life.

Alice ran into his arms. Without hesitation Babbity got down on one knee and asked: "Will you marry me?"

The other customers burst into applause as the happy couple embraced each other.

As they sat down for a coffee Babbity said: "You know my dear, I have seen many things on my travels that told me life is too short. I began to realise I didn't want to be apart from you again.

"I'm so happy," he added.

"Me too," replied Alice

CHAPTER 12

Last piece of the jigsaw

In the days, weeks and months that followed, Babbity visited Ruth's brother and formed a great friendship.

He also met up a few times with Father John, explaining the deliverance experience to him in detail.

The priest said the particulars of Babbity's deliverance work would be referred to the local bishop for consensus and, hopefully, approval.

Babbity also reported back to PC Baxter and gave him a full resume of what happened in Krakow.

Six months later Babbity completed his RCIA course and was accepted into the Catholic Church.

He and Alice were married by Father John in Saint Mary's Church - approximately four weeks after his induction.

On that glorious summer's day friends and relatives attended the wedding, including Ruth's brother Rabbi David Goldberg and Alice's sister Sheila who was accompanied by her parents.

Babbity was sure he could feel the presence of his father Aaron too.

His thoughts strayed to the events of the last two years. "Wow" he thought.

He then noticed Father John winking at him.

Babbity smiled contentedly.

That single wink of the eye was the sign that his life had now changed forever.

Babbity knew in his heart, his adventure with God had only just begun.

The End

ACKNOWLEDGEMENTS

To Mathew Lynch (Editor) Former Production Editor and Cheif Sub Editor - The Sunday Times - Scotland
A big thank you Matt , for your dedicated help.

To all people I have met on my spiritual journey - without you I am nothing.

*He was made visible in the flesh
attested by the spirit
seen by angels
proclaimed by the pagans
believed in by the world
taken up in glory.*

1 Timothy 3 v 14-16

www.ingramcontent.com/pod-product-compliance
Lightning Source LLC
Chambersburg PA
CBHW081344070526
44578CB00005B/717